LIVING CONNECTED
EXPERIENCING HEALTHY FAMILY ON MISSION

Russell D. Cravens

LUCIDBOOKS

LIVING CONNECTED
Experiencing Healthy Family on Mission
Copyright © 2017 by Russell D. Cravens

Published by Lucid Books in Houston, TX
www.LucidBooksPublishing.com

All rights reserved. No part of this publication may be reproduced, stored in a retrieval system, or transmitted in any form by any means, electronic, mechanical, photocopy, recording, or otherwise, without the prior permission of the publisher, except as provided for by USA copyright law.

Unless otherwise noted, Scripture quotations are from the ESV® Bible (The Holy Bible, English Standard Version®), copyright © 2001 by Crossway, a publishing ministry of Good News Publishers. Used by permission. All rights reserved.

Scripture quotations marked (NIV) are taken from the Holy Bible, New International Version®, NIV®. Copyright © 1973, 1978, 1984, 2011 by Biblica, Inc.™ Used by permission of Zondervan. All rights reserved worldwide. www.zondervan.com The "NIV" and "New International Version" are trademarks registered in the United States Patent and Trademark Office by Biblica, Inc.™

Scripture quotations marked (NLT) are taken from the Holy Bible, New Living Translation, copyright ©1996, 2004, 2007, 2013, 2015 by Tyndale House Foundation. Used by permission of Tyndale House Publishers, Inc., Carol Stream, Illinois 60188. All rights reserved.

ISBN-10: 1-63296-173-3
ISBN-13: 978-1-63296-173-0
eISBN-10: 1-63296-174-1
eISBN-13: 978-1-63296-174-7

Special Sales: Most Lucid Books titles are available in special quantity discounts. Custom imprinting or excerpting can also be done to fit special needs. Contact Lucid Books at Info@LucidBooksPublishing.com.

Table of Contents

Chapter 1: Introduction: Living Connected on Mission   1

Chapter 2: Living Connected & Anger   19

Chapter 3: Living Connected & Words   37

Chapter 4: Living Connected & Conflict   53

Chapter 5: Living Connected & Touch   71

Chapter 6: Living Connected & Money   91

Chapter 7: Living Connected & Rest   113

Summary and Invitation to Mission   133

Notes   143

Special Thanks

"Writing a book is an adventure. To begin with it is a toy and an amusement. Then it becomes a mistress, then it becomes a master, then it becomes a tyrant. The last phase is that just as you are about to be reconciled to your servitude, you kill the monster and fling him to the public."

—Winston S. Churchill

The ideas I attempt to capture with words in this book are a small part of a larger story God is writing. I am a part of that story, and my story overlaps so many others. Along the way, I have been fortunate to make many incredible friends, learn from wise mentors, and grow through leading people. I'd like to thank everyone who has impacted my life and, as a result, added to the writing that I now fling to the public.

I am grateful for the faithful, loving influence of my parents. Chris and Edwina, you are the most steady, selfless, and loving people I know. I want you to know that your Christian witness is being multiplied through me to many people. I dedicate this book to you.

I am grateful for the people of Neartown Church. Specifically, I am deeply indebted to those of you who have partnered with me from day one of this daring, risky step of faith to give our lives more fully to the mission of God in the inner city of Houston. This book is for you.

I am most grateful for my own family. To my kids, I've written this book with you in mind. There is no one in the world more important to me as I consider the mission of God. Although it will be some years before you really understand the ideas put forth in this book, I want you to know that my greatest passion in this life is to lovingly father you as we walk together on mission with God.

To Jeanie, my best friend and soul mate. You have lived the ideas on these pages more than anyone else. You have patiently, lovingly walked alongside me as I have had to learn so much about myself, being a husband and dad, and leading others. I am grateful for you. This book is for you.

CHAPTER 1

Introduction:
Living Connected on Mission

Life is short. There is nothing really profound about this statement, and I am sure you have heard it before. But, the older I get, the more I realize how important it is to be gripped by that reality. I have, on more than one occasion, held the hand of a person in their last moments of life. I have, on more than one occasion, hugged those who grieved the death of someone they loved dearly. Every single time, I am awakened anew to how fleeting and fragile and temporary our lives are on earth. With that comes the painful reality that the time I have as a husband and dad is fleeting. I don't want to waste a day of my life. I don't want to miss an opportunity to live life to the fullest. So, I frequently ask God for focus and direction so that my time on earth is well spent. And what I am learning is that I can best spend my time joining in with

God on his mission. It's impossible to predict how many days we have remaining, but recently I did some research and discovered with 75 percent accuracy I will live to be at least 86 years old.[1] If this is true, I am almost halfway through my days on earth. Crazy. I want to make the most of every one of them.

I imagine most of you have heard a preacher say something like this: "God is doing something in the world, and he invites you to be a part of it!" Or maybe it went something like this: "You are the hands and feet of Jesus!" Or perhaps you read something like this before: "But whatever you do, find the God-centered, Christ-exalting, Bible-saturated passion of your life, and find your way to say it and live for it and die for it. And you will make a difference that lasts. You will not waste your life."[2]

We walk out of church believing our lives were meant for something great, but nothing changes. The reason nothing changes is not because we don't believe God can use us, but because we are living disconnected. We are disconnected from ourselves and others in our homes. If connections in our home aren't strengthened, the passion to be used by God for his glory will fade by Monday. For many, it's the same routine every week.

I am writing with the strong assumption that every Christian is most alive when they are on mission with God. And, what makes this life even more fulfilling is when we learn to connect in healthy ways with others in our families so we can live on mission together.

Some years ago, the language of "living missional" was introduced to Christian church life. It is now quite common to hear people talk about missional communities, missional lifestyle, mission statements, mission . . . whatever. But it seems to me that figuring out God's mission and how to get in on it has become far too complicated. Here is what I do know: I have one life to live. I have one wife. I have one set of kids. Surely, I will make mistakes, but one mistake I won't make is neglecting the invitation from God to get in on what he is doing in the world.

The apostle Paul writes so powerfully about the mission of God through people when he says that anyone who belongs to Christ has become a new person. The old life is gone; a new life has begun! All of this is a gift from God, who brought us back to himself through Christ, and God has given us this task of reconciling people to him. For God was in Christ, reconciling the world to himself, no longer counting people's sins against them. And he gave us this wonderful message of reconciliation (2 Corinthians 5:17–19).

That is a mission to live for—and (if God so chooses) to die for. Living for anything that you are also willing to die for is the best way I know to live fully alive.

The Bible as the Starting Point

The Bible is filled with stories of families invited by God to live on mission. Along the way, there are some epic moments when the family leader stands tall and declares a commitment to be all about the mission of God. I love these stories, and I want to take you on a journey through one of them. I hope it inspires you to commit to God's mission in a similar way. Joshua is one of the great family leaders talked about in the Bible. I love the way he invites all the people he leads to assess their commitment to the mission of God and declares his own intent in Joshua 24:15: "*As for me and my house, we will serve the Lord.*"

My hope in the following chapters is to help you live connected with others in your family so that you can do what we all must do in response to what God has done. As we look at a story in Joshua 24 about Joshua's catalytic speech to Israel, think about how this idea of mission relates to your own family. Notice how Joshua lays things out for the people of Israel. First, he describes their situation *before God*. Then, he reminds them what God has done—*but God*. Finally, he answers the question, "*What must we do?*" My hope is that your heart will be more fully gripped with a sense of mission so that you are willing to work toward healthy connections in your home.

The Squandered Mission: Before God

> *¹Joshua gathered all the tribes of Israel to Shechem and summoned the elders, the heads, the judges, and the officers of Israel. And they presented themselves before God. ²And Joshua said to all the people, "Thus says the Lord, the God of Israel, 'Long ago, your fathers lived beyond the Euphrates, Terah, the father of Abraham and of Nahor; and they served other gods.'"*

To set the scene for you, this is the last major event in Joshua's life. If you are new to the Bible and are not familiar with Joshua, you may remember Moses, who led the Israelites out of slavery in Egypt and received the law of God on Mount Sinai. Well, Joshua was Moses' successor, who took over leading Israel after Moses died.

A bit more background — Israel is God's chosen people, descendants of Abraham. Abraham was a worshiper of false gods, but God chose Abraham and began to make himself known through a special relationship held together with promises that God made. In the passage of Joshua 24, we find Joshua with Israel at this significant place in their nation's history — Shechem, the same place God had called Abraham. Joshua calls all of the people together to tell them that there was a time when they were not a family who honored and worshiped God. Joshua calls out their parents . . . and even their grandparents. Seriously, Joshua is calling out "Mimi and Pappa" for wasting their lives.

Have you ever considered how your upbringing ("family of origin") has shaped the way you relate to others as an adult? In the ways that our families were healthy, we tend to be healthy. In the ways that our families were dysfunctional, we also struggle to relate to others in healthy ways. This includes God. Yep, the way we think about God, for better or worse, is most greatly impacted by our relationship with our parents and the way our parents related to God. And, no matter how great our parents were, they were not perfect. Without God entering into our dysfunction, we are going to struggle to live connected to our own families in healthy ways. And, if we cannot relate in healthy ways to others in our home, we will neglect the mission of God and waste our lives.

Let's look at what happens when God enters into the family.

The Missionary God

> ³"'Then I took your father Abraham from beyond the River and led him through all the land of Canaan, and made his offspring many. I gave him Isaac. ⁴And to Isaac I gave Jacob and Esau. And I gave Esau the hill country of Seir to possess, but Jacob and his children went down to Egypt. ⁵And I sent Moses and Aaron, and I plagued Egypt with what I did in the midst of it, and afterward I brought you out. ⁶Then I brought your fathers out of Egypt, and you came to the sea. And the Egyptians pursued your fathers with chariots and horsemen to the Red Sea. ⁷And when they cried to the Lord, he put darkness between you and the Egyptians and made the sea come upon them and cover them; and your eyes saw what I did in Egypt. And you lived in the wilderness a long time. ⁸Then I brought you to the land of the Amorites, who lived on the other side of the Jordan. They fought with you, and I gave them into your hand, and you took possession of their land, and I destroyed them before you.'"

These eighteen "then I..." statements tell an in-depth family history for Israel. The Lord reminds his people of all the times he multiplied them and gave them lands to inhabit, and the times they cried out to him and he rescued them.

When writers in the Old Testament want to talk about the awesome power of God, they often refer back to an event called the "Exodus." To fill you in, at one point in history, the Israelites were enslaved to the Egyptians for

INTRODUCTION: LIVING CONNECTED ON MISSION

400 years. Israel cried out and begged God to rescue his people, and finally God sent a deliverer—Moses. Moses confronted the Egyptian Pharaoh, and God used Moses to lead his own people out of slavery to take them into the land he had promised them. Joshua tells this story to remind the Israelites that God has done something that no earthly power can do.

God declares through Joshua, "I have done awesome things in your life, and it wasn't by your power or by your bow." Think back on your own life. *What was it like before God entered my life, and what has it been like since God took hold of my life?*

If you think for a moment that your success in business, or your beautiful family, or your academic achievements, or your influence, or whatever other success you have, is because of your sword and your bow—in other words, your own strength—then you're fooling yourself. It is only by the grace of God that you adapted in this world and are able to function as an adult.

God has done some awesome things in our lives. He has delivered all of us from deep, dark places of sin. When we were wallowing in that sin, enjoying it, believing that the sin could meet our needs or desires, God in his love and grace and mercy thought of us, rescued us, and brought us to a place of freedom. Verse 13 describes how God has done this for Israel: "I gave you a land on which you had not labored and cities that you had not built. You dwell in them, and you eat of the fruit of the vineyards and olive orchards that you did not plant."

The good things in our lives—God did them all. The food we eat, the job we work to make the money we spend—all of those things are gifts from God. If that hurts to hear, then this should be a heart check for you.

If you forget that it's by the grace of God alone that you have anything good in your life, then you will care little about the things that God cares about in this life. Israel had to understand that their success wasn't from their own strength—it was from God. You and I have to get this too if we want to lead our families to join in the mission of God.

When our understanding of how glorious God is grows higher and higher, and our understanding of our own desperate need for God grows deeper and deeper, something happens. Our appreciation for what Jesus has done to reconcile us to God becomes greater. And, we become even more willing to declare allegiance to God while prioritizing our lives around the things that God most cares about in this life.

Do you hear the sound of God's victory anymore? Does the story of the missionary God who broke into your darkness bring light to your face and joy to your life? Unfortunately, too many of us have been lulled to sleep by the dull noise of me-centric Christianity. At first, you loved it: church programs for you, sermons for you, and songs for you. You had your basic belief: Jesus died for your sin so you could get to go to heaven. But, now you are asleep spiritually and your entire life is passing you by with no real zeal for the mission of God.

I don't want to live like this. It's boring. I want to be the one snapping my fingers above your face, pleading with you to open your eyes to see what God wants you to see. I imagine Joshua doing this in the story. "Israel! Your Pappa and Mimi were pagans. You grew up in a

INTRODUCTION: LIVING CONNECTED ON MISSION

situation that was broken!" *Joshua snaps his fingers.* "But, God rescued you!" *Joshua snaps his fingers again.* "So, let's decide today if the mission of God matters!"

His Mission Is Our Mission: Serve God

> *¹⁴"Now therefore fear the L*ORD *and serve him in sincerity and in faithfulness. Put away the gods that your fathers served beyond the River and in Egypt, and serve the L*ORD*. ¹⁵And if it is evil in your eyes to serve the L*ORD*, choose this day whom you will serve, whether the gods your fathers served in the region beyond the River, or the gods of the Amorites in whose land you dwell. But as for me and my house, we will serve the L*ORD*."*

After reminding them of the reality of their family of origin when their parents did not worship God, and then reminding them of the way that God rescued them from slavery, Joshua calls them to respond to the mission of God.

I love this moment in the story. For those people still listening to Joshua, it did not matter what they experienced as a child or what they did as an adult up to this point. All that mattered was that one moment when Joshua was calling them into serving the Lord. He didn't pressure them; if they wanted to serve the false gods of their fathers, they were free to go and do as they pleased.

You may have parents who related to God only on Sundays at church. I was fortunate to grow up in a home with a mom and stepdad who loved the Bible and prioritized church. But, we didn't fully comprehend that God could use our family on mission to impact others.

You may have grown up in a home that cared little about the mission of God in the world. You may have even had a bad experience as a child that now tempts you to believe God can't use you. My sense is that most people can look back on their upbringing and bring to mind some way that they began believing they were unusable. How does your background affect the way you relate to others today? An important part of fully engaging the ideas in this book will be to consider your family of origin.

Maybe you feel disconnected from others in your home, and you feel like it's impossible to be used by God on mission. The amazing thing about God is that when he enters into our story, there is no reason that our family of origin or our current difficulty in connecting with others has to keep us from his mission. But, you must choose it. Only you can choose to step into the mission of God. I am begging you to wake up and do it because the world needs Christians who are wide awake, living connected to one another on mission with God.

You might say, "I'm awake. What do I do next?" Joshua is quite clear about what it means for people to be on mission: "serve the Lord!" Serving God involves fearing him, turning from our idols, and turning off cruise control.

Fear the Lord

First, fear the Lord. This idea can be challenging to comprehend because often I tend to think about fear like how I dread a criminal harming me or my family—I often fear what is evil, broken, or dangerous. My default fear is the kind of fear that drives me away from things. But Joshua is not talking about this kind of fear.

INTRODUCTION: LIVING CONNECTED ON MISSION

Joshua is speaking of a fear that is like what I hope my children feel toward me. It's a reverent fear that recognizes authority and strength. They know that when I speak to them, or when I give them *that look*, or when I raise my voice, it's not out of hostility but out of love and care for them. This is a fear laced with love, grace, and mercy. We fear God not because we're afraid he's going to do something harmful to us, but because we know he is awesome and wise and powerful. This kind of fear draws us in. I think this is the kind of fear that Joshua has in mind. And, when we are near God, every other idol has to go.

Turn from Idols

A second prerequisite to living connected on mission is for the Israelites to put away other gods. This isn't the first time Israel listened to one of their leaders say, "You need to put away the gods. Choose today whom you'll serve." I don't know about you, but this is true for me, too. There are times more often than I'd like to admit when I have had to choose to serve the Lord and put away gods.

For Israel, it may have been literal gods, actual objects made out of wood that they worshiped because the neighboring nations worshiped this way. Today we worship false gods differently. It is more subtle because we do not carve a wooden statue and bow down before it. If you need a hint as to what gods are in your life, ask yourself:

- What do I look to do when I am feeling down?
- How do I respond when I am hurt?
- What brings me joy when I am unhappy?
- Where do I seek comfort?

It could be alcohol. It could be sex. It could be a sports team. It could be shopping or passive entertainment. Put away the worship of those things. They are false and will distract you from serving the Lord.

Turn off Cruise Control
There is an echo throughout the people: *"We will serve the Lord"* (v. 18). The people respond to Joshua's wake-up call, and they have a moment of clarity. They remember who God is and what he has done for them, and they know he is worthy of their devotion.

Joshua has made his case, and the people are totally on board. If I were in Joshua's shoes, at this point I would have said, "Hey, that's awesome. I love you. Let's pray together." Instead, Joshua says, "No, you won't" (v. 19). Joshua actually tells the people they are not able to faithfully serve God. They insist, "Yes, we will!" (v. 21).

Guess what. They don't. They end up turning away from God again. Joshua is right—they can't. Our sinful default is to turn on cruise control and to drift back to idolatry.

My Story

Somewhere along the way, God graciously captured my attention. The more I hear stories like Joshua declaring, "as for me and my house, we will serve the Lord," the more passionate I become to lead my family to do the same. But, passion is not enough. I have learned that much of what is required for healthy relationships is to be honest about who we have become. And, who we are is most impacted by our experiences as children.

INTRODUCTION: LIVING CONNECTED ON MISSION

If you choose to let me lead you through these following chapters, let me warn you—you will be reminded of ways that your upbringing has not been great. Like Joshua is reminding Israel of their past, you will be reminded of yours. Of course, you will also experience joy as you remember the ways your childhood was good. In my experience, the difficulties people experience in current family relationships are most impacted by not so great experiences they had as children. The way you show up in every relationship today is most heavily influenced by what you experienced as a child. Whoever raised you did so imperfectly, and experiencing a healthy family will require you to recognize the ways it impacted you.

I feel grateful for my upbringing. But, it was not perfect. My parents divorced when I was young. My father was in the Army and stationed in Germany when I was born. Not long after I was born, he decided he would rather live single than be married to my mom and take care of my sister and me. We lived with him in Germany at the time, so he brought my mom, my sister, and me back to Florida and essentially said, "Okay, you're on your own." We made our way back to Oklahoma and stayed with family. As a child, this affected me deeply. Looking back, I realize my heart was traumatized by abandonment from my father. This is just one of the multiple things I experienced during my upbringing that impacted the way I learned how to express anger, use my words, express love with touch, and every other thing I will write about in the chapters that follow. I grew up with this brokenness within me—brokenness I wasn't even aware of.

By God's grace, my mom remarried a Godly man whom I could learn to love as a dad. This kept me from growing up completely fatherless, but this didn't heal the deep wounds I experienced as a child. Over time, I discovered that the wounds I experienced as a child affected the way that I show up in relationships. And, it has impacted the way I connect with the Heavenly Father. Remember, as adults we carry adapted childhood patterns of behavior into the relationships we have with our spouses, our boyfriends or girlfriends, or our kids. For me, that deep wound of abandonment is something I still deal with to this day. It was a part of my early formation. The way this has played out for me, as an adult, is that I tend to exhaust myself striving toward perfection to prove in some way to God, myself, and others that I should never have been abandoned. Honestly, it is the primary reason I still struggle to resist temptations that lead to sin.

As I looked at those things, I began to think about how they affect the way I express anger or the way I deal with conflict. I began to think about the way I use my words, the way I think about the relationship I have with money. Ultimately, these things affect the way I relate to my wife, my kids, and my church. But God is transforming these areas. God has been doing something in me, and I hope that as you consider how you have been shaped by your upbringing, you will invite God to transform you.

Listen carefully: God can use you in his mission to help others. But, it will require you to get honest about your own story and let the work of Jesus Christ in your life transform the patterns of unhealthy connection. For you to connect with others in your home in healthy ways will require a supernatural work of God in your heart. It won't be easy, but living in any other way would be a waste of the precious mission God invites your family into.

The Gospel and Living Connected

This is why Jesus came.

Even with all the inspiring speeches and compelling calls by leaders like Joshua, Israel could not stay on mission. They continued to drift again and again. Maybe you, like the Israelites, find yourself wanting to commit to the Lord but seem unable to keep from serving other gods. And, maybe you feel beat down by this reality. I want to encourage you that the fact that Israel and you are unable to serve the Lord perfectly is the very reason that God became flesh in the form of the man we call Jesus. And, the reason God, the Father, chose that God, the Son, would be crucified was so that our sins can be forgiven. In some ironic way, the frequent missteps in our efforts to fully serve the Lord are the greatest illustration of why we need Jesus. And, the only way our hearts can transform, enabling us to live deeply connected on mission, is through Jesus. When you believe this good news, you are ready to serve the Lord and lead your family on mission.

I hope this inspires you. Life is short. Let's be like Joshua, boldly setting direction for our families and declaring, "As for me and my house, we will serve the Lord." I believe that most of you reading this want to honor God with your time on earth and live on mission for him. And, in my experience, the greatest limiter for you will be relational difficulties within your home that distract you from the mission of God. In nearly every situation, the problem is that one or multiple persons need help in the most basic areas to develop healthy relationships.

In the chapters that follow, we'll look at six common roadblocks that keep families from living on mission with God. The roadblocks are poorly handled anger, careless words, unhealthy conflict, withholding loving touch, mismanaged money, and neglected rest. We will look at each of these through the lens of the gospel while asking God to transform how we approach each of these basic family challenges. Why? Because life is too short to let these areas keep us from fully participating in the mission of God.

Reflection Questions

- What was your purpose in life like before God entered your life?

_____

_____

_____

- How did your family of origin affect your goals in life (past and present)?

_____

_____

_____

INTRODUCTION: LIVING CONNECTED ON MISSION

- What has your mission been like since God took hold of your life? Would your next-door neighbor agree with that assessment?

  _____
  _____
  _____
  _____
  _____

- Explain the following statement in your own words: "In some ironic way, the frequent missteps in our efforts to fully serve the Lord are the greatest illustration of why we need Jesus."

  _____
  _____
  _____
  _____
  _____

- How does sin keep your family from living on mission together?

  _____
  _____
  _____
  _____

- Your lost coworker is discouraged because his family is chaotically running in different directions. How would this chapter inform what you would tell him?

CHAPTER 2

Living Connected & Anger

Outbursts disrupt peace in the home. As a parent to four children, I am learning that one of the more important and difficult challenges in the home is helping my kids process anger. Some of what makes it difficult for us as adults to help our kids process anger is that we are not naturally great at dealing with our own anger. I want my kids to grow up knowing two things about their daddy: there are times when Dad gets angry about the right things, and there are also times when he gets angry about the wrong things. But in the times when he gets it wrong, he is willing to ask for forgiveness. Here is what I hope you will understand: the way we process anger will contribute to the degree the people in our home feel connected to one another. And, the more deeply connected you are to one another, the healthier your family will be as you engage the mission of God.

You don't have to drive long in a city like Houston before you encounter an adult set off into rage by another driver. I have been there. Just recently, I was cut off in traffic by another driver, and I became filled with anger. I flashed my lights and honked my horn repeatedly. If they had stopped, I was fully ready for fisticuffs. As I whipped back around them, I am ashamed to say the driver was a little old lady. Yep, I was going to fight someone's grandma. Now, this story is terribly embarrassing, but it reveals what I believe is true about many adults. We need God to transform our hearts so that we process anger in healthy ways. If not, anger will disrupt connection in our homes. Ultimately, anger will create unhealthy fear in our homes, hindering zeal for the mission of God. The main idea of this chapter is this: anger happens, but with God's help we can keep it from hurting relationships with those we love.

Anger manifests itself in different ways. You may have heard the terminology "fight or flight," which describes two main reactions to anger: running away or going into battle. Either way, anger has the potential to destroy your family relationships. Not only can anger hurt relationships, but anger can also affect your health. According to a study done by European cardiologists, anger can increase your risk of heart attacks.[1] In fact, within two hours of an outburst of anger, a person's chances of a heart or stroke skyrocket. If you are unable to process anger, not only will it kill the relationships important to you, but it can also kill you. Anger is a killer, and we need help.

Scripture and the Problem of Anger

So what does the Bible say we should do about anger? The book of James is a letter written to a fledgling church. The letter contains numerous short, punchy statements of truth for the young believers reading it. In verse 1:19–20, James addresses the issue of anger, saying, "Know this, my beloved brothers: let every person be quick to hear, slow to speak, slow to anger; for the anger of man does not produce the righteousness of God."

The apostle Paul also talks about anger in his letter to the Ephesians. He says in Ephesians 4:26–27, "Be angry and do not sin; do not let the sun go down on your anger and give no opportunity to the devil." In verse 31, he calls his readers to "let all bitterness and wrath and anger and clamor and slander be put away from you, along with all malice." The Book of Ecclesiastes says it this way: "Do not be quickly provoked in your spirit for anger resides in the lap of fools" (7:9 NIV)

These verses make several big statements about anger. First, not all anger is harmful. James says, "be slow to anger," insinuating that there are times when it's quite natural to be angry. The fact that certain things make you angry does not mean there's something wrong with you. In fact, on more than one occasion Jesus got angry. So not all anger is harmful, but we also know that not all anger is beneficial.

Anger can be destructive. For couples to build healthy marriages, anger unchecked can be far more devastating than sexual sin or financial stress. It's a big deal.

The line that we need to find is how to feel anger and process it without sinning. We need to capture what Paul means when he writes, *"In your anger do not sin"* (Eph. 4:26 NIV). We must think carefully about how we can get angry about the right things and, when we're angry about the wrong things, how we can process our anger in a way that is helpful and draws us closer to the ones we love instead of dividing us.

Family and the Problem of Anger

Learning how to handle anger is one of the most important tasks of parenting. Often, parents teach their children that anger is bad. Ironically, anger is also the means by which these parents discipline their children, essentially sending this message: "I'm going to get really mad at you because you continue to be angry with each other." The more time I spend in counseling situations, the more I encounter people who have never learned to deal with their anger. Since becoming a pastor, I have been the officiant at hundreds of weddings. Prior to these ceremonies I usually do premarital counseling with the couple. Typically, I spend the most time trying to understand what it was like for each person in the home they grew up in. Again, our family of origin influences how we learn to show up in the world as adults. My inquiry includes reflective exercises like, "Try to remember a time when you got in trouble at school. It was enough that your teacher reported what happened to your parents." (Of course, there are some of you who never got in trouble at school, so just make up a scenario in your head. I got in trouble frequently, so it's an exercise that makes sense to me.) I then ask the following questions:

- What happened when your parents got home?
- What did your mom do?
- What did your dad do?
- Did anyone yell at you?

- Did your dad handle the discipline? Your mom?
- When your parents got mad at you, what happened?
- More broadly, when your parents got mad at one another, what happened?

Often, this exercise reveals patterns of dealing with anger that inform the way each person will deal with anger in their own marriage. Almost always, I learn that one parent overreacted (fight) and one parent under-reacted (flight) as a way of processing angry moments. Rarely do I meet a couple whose parents dealt with anger in a balanced, calm manner. It is always my hope to help the couple identify patterns of dealing with anger in unhealthy ways so they can develop a healthy connection with one another.

I also counsel couples who've been married for several years. Sadly, I am usually trying to help them deal with the wounds caused by patterns of dysfunction in how they deal with anger. I think of one couple, Bill and Margaret. Bill grew up in a home with a dad who came home from work each day angry and then sat on a couch and drank himself to sleep. While watching TV, Bill's dad would blare music insanely loudly to drown out every other sound.

I asked Bill, "Can you remember a time when your dad talked to you about your day?"

"No."

"Well, what did he do when you got into trouble or needed discipline?"

Bill's eyes filled with tears. He didn't answer. He didn't have to. As I looked over to his beautiful wife, I began to see the sadness in her own eyes as, no doubt, she recalled times in their young marriage when Bill dealt with her harshly. God help us. How are these two supposed to start a family that declares, "For me and my house, we will serve the Lord"? They are consumed with the strife that comes from Bill's dysfunction in handling his anger. But in order to become an emotionally healthy adult, you must learn to deal with anger.

Consider why you get angry. I get angry because my football team didn't play the right quarterback, or that store didn't have my size, or that person cut me off in traffic. But I don't think that any of these things are the real issue. The real reason we get angry about things has to do with love. Anger is a natural response to a threat toward someone or something we love. If we love the wrong things, it will be impossible to handle anger appropriately. Bill gets angry when he feels out of control because he secretly loves control. It gives him a sense of order in his disordered heart. But only God can bring order to his heart.

Jesus and the Essence of Anger

There are good reasons to get angry. I mentioned already that Jesus got angry. One example appears in Mark chapter three, and that story can help us to think about an instance where it might be okay to be angry. The story begins in Mark 3:1. Jesus enters the synagogue[2] and meets a man there who has a withered hand. This was not uncommon. Sick people would gather around the religious buildings in hopes that they would receive help from the religious people there.

Meanwhile, the Pharisees watch Jesus. In Jesus's time, the Pharisees were religious leaders who Jesus frequently accused of having an external religiosity, but had hearts far from God—they looked really religious, but they were dead spiritually. In this instance, the Pharisees are watching Jesus to see whether he will heal this sick man on the Sabbath. The Sabbath is a weekly day of rest God instituted in the Old Testament meant to help people more fully worship God. The problem with the Pharisees during this time is that it had become more about the rules and less about devotion to God.

Jesus walks into the synagogue on this Sabbath, and the Pharisees are there, along with this ill man. The Pharisees are watching Jesus. He is under investigation by the Pharisees as to whether or not he is going to heal on the Sabbath day—a day where you're not supposed to do work. Jesus knows they are there to accuse him, so he calls over the sick man and in verse four says to the Pharisees, "Is it lawful on the Sabbath to do good or to do harm, to save life or to kill?" The Pharisees are silent.

Jesus knows their hearts. He knows that something is broken inside of them. They are more concerned about whether or not he's going to follow this religious rule than they are concerned about this man who is ill and needs help. And so Jesus is angry. It's moments like this in the Bible when we really see the humanity of Jesus. Scripture says that Jesus is grieved at the hardness of their hearts (Mark 3:5).

But Jesus tells the man to stretch out his hand. The man stretches his hand out, and immediately it is restored.

Why was Jesus angry? Because the behavior of the Pharisees was a threat to the wellbeing of this person Jesus loved. Jesus loves people, and the Pharisees were more concerned with Jesus's religion than this man's needs.

Jesus's love for people was offended. Jesus's anger was completely justified because he loved the right things, and when those things were offended, he became angry.

I remember a time recently when I got really angry for good reason. I live in a home on a narrow, one-way street with no sidewalks. If someone wants to quickly get through the neighborhood, they sometimes risk driving the wrong way down my street. When my kids are playing out in front, if somebody goes the wrong way down this one-way street, it's very dangerous. Recently, my kindergarten-aged son was playing in the street when a car turned the wrong way down the street and quickly endangered the safety of my son. So, I jumped in front of the car and stood my ground, not allowing the car to continue down the one-way street. They got angry. I got angry. Their anger was at me because of their love for convenience (even if it endangers another). My anger (completely justified) bubbled up because of my love for my son. This person's actions endangered my son, and I was furious. But I wanted them to understand that they'd made me angry because the safety of my children, whom I love, was threatened.

Disordered Affections

Maybe you get angry when you hear about things that are happening in our world. You may get angry when you see injustices happening in your city. But if most of us are honest, most of the time we get angry about much less important things. We get angry when our conveniences are disrupted or when people say things that rub us the wrong way. In our homes, we get angry when we feel out of control. We get angry when we have not rested and are over-tired. We get angry, ultimately, because we love the wrong things. These things cause us to lash out. The reason is that in our humanity, we tend to love the wrong things.

St. Augustine, an influential early church theologian, calls these wrong things our inordinate affections.[3] I've also heard it called disordered love. As humans, we tend to love the wrong things, and we get angry when those things are threatened. Consequently, we behave in ways that hinder our connections with other people.

I want to give you a couple of examples to get you thinking about how this affects your family. In family life, there are two things that we really, really love. We love to be in control, and we love our reputations. When we feel a loss of control or we get a bad reputation, we become angry.

Affection for Control

In marriage, we love control. Often, when one or both parties are angry, it's because they are frustrated that they cannot control the other person. When the other person does not behave, either doing or not doing something that we want them to do or not do, it stirs anger within us. We get angry because our control has been threatened.

What happens next is fight or flight—and often whether or not you fight or flee depends on what your parents modeled for you when you were a child. We fight with harsh words, or maybe even more dangerously, we fight with passive-aggressive behavior.

Maybe you are more prone to flight. Some of the ways we flee are by letting that anger smolder beneath the surface and distancing ourselves, disengaging from family life, or busying ourselves with work and recreation. This creates separation, hinders intimacy, kills communication, and leads to an empty, lifeless marriage. It's impossible to live connected on mission with God in this kind of marriage.

Affection for Reputation

This also applies to parenting. Often, the reason we become angry as parents is because we love our reputations. We want people to think we are good parents, and when our kids do something that reflects negatively on our parenting, we get angry—angrier than we should. Maybe you remember doing something as a child that really wasn't a huge deal, but one or both of your parents flew off the handle about it. It may, in fact, have been that their reputation was offended.

Having children is sanctifying work. It can really bust up your reputation, especially if you're the type of person who likes to have everything in order at all times. All of us like to manage people's impressions of us at some level. When you have kids, though, it is impossible to always manage others' impressions of you.

Your reputation is on the line any time you go anywhere with your kids. Any time you let your kids into the play area at Chick-fil-A, you put your reputation on the line. I guarantee you that the way the children behave will affect everybody else's impression about whether or not that parent is good. Humorously, that's one reason I don't like to go to Chick-fil-A—I don't want to be associated with any misbehavior.

As I mentioned, when our kids misbehave, sometimes our love of our own reputation causes us to overreact and say things we don't mean. But maybe even more dangerous is when other adults insinuate that we're not good parents, making us feel we're losing our reputation. It happens, and sometimes it causes us to parent on the edge of anger at all times.

Here's an example from my own life. I enjoy sports, and thankfully I have kids who enjoy being active. I am well aware of the kind of parenting that places unfair pressure on children to become star athletes. Often, parents are trying to live vicariously through their kids. I started out intent on not becoming this type of parent.

Don't get me wrong—I would love it if one of my kids did well enough in sports to play in college or even professionally, but the likelihood is infinitesimally small. Reality is, however, that I love my own reputation. At times, I have believed the lie that how well my kids do on their team either builds or kills my good reputation as a great dad.

Recently, at a football practice, one of my kids was proving to be one of the weaker players. And, I got angry at him. In my mind, he was not trying hard enough, and he was a complete waste of money and time by being out there. Concerned that my child wasn't doing well because I was too soft as a dad, I asked him in anger, "Do you think I tell you too often how much I love you?" In truth, I was already having a hard time connecting with these new dads, and without a superstar athlete, I felt I would never be liked by them. (I fully expect you to quit reading this book; seriously, how can anyone who says a thing like this be trusted.) I left the event angry. I was fuming as I drove home. And, my son could sense I was angry at him. He sat quietly, trying not to do anything that might release the pressure building in my words. I felt so much anger, I didn't even want to enter my own house. Instead, I dropped my kids off at home, and then I did what every right-thinking man does when he gets angry: I went to Lowe's.

One of my mentors made me promise him that any time I experienced emotions that I was struggling to process, I would call him. So, I called him, right there in Lowe's. I won't tell you everything that was said in that conversation, but it ended with me sitting down in the tool section, crying. Talk about a reputation killer. I was crying at Lowe's—in the tool section. So weird. You see, I am just now learning to process anger. Yep, I am a grown man, employed by a Christian church, and I struggle to process anger in healthy ways. What I realized in that moment was that my anger was a secondary emotion covering a deeper emotion, which was my love for my own reputation. My own self-love and my desire for people to see me in a certain way caused me to become angry. I hated the feeling of being perceived as an ineffective dad, unable to teach my own son how to play sports. In Lowe's, I realized how crazy it was to think that expressing love to my son would make him less of a man. I was stunned by how a disordered love for my own reputation could stir such anger. I left Lowe's and went directly home to embrace my son, asking forgiveness while telling him repeatedly, "I love you."

How the Gospel Reorders Our Affections

What do you love so much that it moves you to the kind of anger that would be embarrassing to admit? Maybe it's a love of reputation or a love of control. Whatever it is, you will find your identity in things you love the most. And if you love anything more than Jesus, you'll put your identity in that thing. You'll get angry when that thing is threatened, and then you'll get angry about all the wrong things.

Maybe this resonates with you, and you want to know what steps to take toward actually controlling your anger. In order for your heart to be changed to love something other than yourself, you must come to a place where you realize your need for God. And that connection with God is only possible when you submit your angry heart to Jesus Christ.

Once you connect with God through Jesus Christ, his Spirit gets inside of you and begins to work on your heart. It doesn't happen overnight. I have followed Christ for a lot of years, and I'm still dealing with disordered affections that result in anger. I still need the gospel of Jesus Christ to transform my heart so that my greatest love is not for myself, my reputation, or my sense of control, but for Jesus.

The Gospel Enables Righteous Anger

If anxiety is rising and the heat in your face is increasing, if you can hear the words coming out of your mouth and they're not words of love toward your spouse or your kids, remove yourself from the situation and think about it. Think about what is making you so angry and ask this question: What do I love that's being offended? What do I love that's being threatened?

Is it control? Is it your reputation? Are you having a hard time managing everybody's impressions of you? If so, consider what you most love. Yourself? Jesus? Take your eyes off of yourself, and put them on God. You're not perfect, and you never will be. You must learn to do this for your family to live connected on mission with God.

Thankfully, there is a kind of anger that moves us to act in ways that honor God. I have in mind a healthy anger about things that threaten God's glory and minimize his love for people. We must let this anger move us to act. Certainly, there are people out there who are angry about things that threaten God's glory and his heart for people, but they are behaving in a way that does not represent how Jesus brought healing. In fact, they are creating more anger and more disconnectedness in our society. So if you're angry about things in your city, things in your home, or things in our world that are a threat to God's glory and his love for people, get angry and do something about it. Get active.

We should get angry about the neglected places in our city. We should get angry like Jesus when he ignored the religious voices telling him not to help people in need. Instead, he acted. He stepped into this guy's life and brought healing. That's the anger that compels us to engage the mission of God. It's not venomous; it's not harmful. It represents Jesus's love and care for people who are in the margins. Those are the things we want to get angry about.

Let's get angry about the right things, and then let's talk about our anger. If you feel that you're getting angry in ways that are not helpful to your marriage or to your parenting, then talk about it. Find somebody you can talk to, just like I did that day at Lowe's. Call up somebody and say, "Hey, you know what, I'm feeling angry and I need to figure out how to work through this."

What we have to do sometimes is bring somebody into the situation who's not emotional about whatever we're thinking about. It could help us think reasonably about it in that moment, and that's okay. Some of you grew up in a home where your parents simply told you not to be angry, and they tried to shut down these affections in you. Now you feel guilty about being angry. Don't feel the guilt, but instead handle it and process it in a way that's helpful in creating connections. Talk about it, talk to God, pray about it, talk to your spouse, talk to a mentor, and talk to a friend. Just talk about it.

The Gospel Enables Meaningful Repentance
Last, we must repent. Ask for forgiveness. When you get angry in a way that is destructive, ask God to change your heart, talk about it, and ask for help. Have the courage to ask for forgiveness from your spouse or even from your kids. I want my kids to grow up knowing that it's okay to mess up, but when we mess up we need to ask for forgiveness. Anger happens, but with God's help we can keep it from hurting relationships with those we love.

Reflection Questions

- Reflect on the following statement. In what ways have you seen this to be true: "For couples to build healthy marriages, anger unchecked can be far more devastating than sexual sin or financial stress"?

_____

_____

_____

- Think through a time when you did something terrible as a child and your parents addressed it. Think about how each of your parents reacted. How were their reactions similar or different from how you react when your spouse or children let you down?

- What's something that really makes you angry? What did Jesus get angry about? How does that compare to the thing that really gets under your skin?

- How would you explain "disordered affections" to a friend who recently got saved?

- Your unsaved buddy at the gym admits to you that he frequently has angry outbursts toward his wife. What counsel would you offer him? How would your counsel be different if he were a believer in your small group?

- What's one way you can tell that Jesus has changed your affections since you became a Christian? Share with someone about this change this week.

CHAPTER 3

Living Connected & Words

Words are powerful. Just recently, I became the parent of a teenager. This new season has caused me to look back over my first 13 years of parenting and ask, "Have I been a good parent?" I am not sure how good I've been, but I know I've tried. As I reflect, one thing is certain: my best and worst days as a parent have been contingent on how I have used my words. With my words, I have spoken life into my wife and kids. Sadly, I can think of more than just a few times my words have hindered healthy connections in my home. For our families to experience healthy connection on mission, we must recognize the power of words in our homes. My focus here will be to help your family experience a peaceful home with connected individuals who can better understand the power of life-giving words.

Words Matter

Did you know that words can literally alter our brains? In their thought provoking book *Words Can Change Your Brain*, Andrew Newberg and Mark Robert Waldman explain, "A single word has the power to influence the expression of genes that regulate physical and emotional stress."[1] Positive words alter the way you are wired and can physiologically strengthen areas like your frontal lobe—the part of your brain that responds and moves to action. Also, negative words can increase the activity in your amygdala—the fear center of the brain. A negative word fires that area of the brain, producing stress hormones, which can interrupt your ability to reason. Words are so powerful they can literally modify the way our brains process information.

I am wondering if you grew up in a home where the world created by words was a place you liked living. Every child needs parents who understand the power of words. Parents who understand the power of words will frequently say:

"I love you more than I ever thought I could love someone."

"You have got what it takes." (I cannot emphasize enough how important this phrase is in your home. This is the question of every child, "Do I have what it takes?")

"I am proud of you."

Take a moment and reflect back on your childhood. How did those in authority over you use their words? Can you remember the frequent use of "I love you" or "I am proud of you"? Or, can you more easily remember harsh rebukes and words of shame? My guess is that you can remember some of both. The way you experienced words as a child is impacting the way you are using them in your home as an adult. Words matter.

The Bible and the Power of Words

The Bible talks frequently about the power of words. As we study the Bible and grow in our faith, we will also grow in learning the best use of our words.

A World of Beauty or a World of Brokenness

> *A word fitly spoken is like apples of gold in a setting of silver.*
> —Proverbs 25:11

Words, rightly spoken, add value in our homes. Some of the imagery in Proverbs 25:11 is lost on us. You probably aren't thinking, "I have that exact thing on my kitchen table." But the author is describing something which, in his time, would have been considered beautiful and precious.

What we know is that words are valuable when they are carefully crafted to strengthen relationships. Words create worlds. If our words are positive and kind and loving, then the world we're creating is a positive and kind and loving atmosphere. If our words are hateful and harmful and ugly, then the world we are creating in our homes will limit healthy connections. Again, words create worlds.

A Sword or a Scalpel

> *There is one whose rash words are like sword thrusts, but the tongue of the wise brings healing.*
> —Proverbs 12:18

The Bible also teaches that words can hurt or heal. There's an old phrase that goes, "Sticks and stones may break my bones, but words will never hurt me." That is simply not true. Words can hurt. They can hurt deeply. Think about words you've spoken to your family in a heated moment, or maybe in a time of stress, when your words left your lips like a sword thrust into the heart of the hearer. Words can wound, but the good news is that the same tool can also be an instrument of healing. If you can think of a time in your life when somebody said something to you that was positive, encouraging, or kind, or when someone gave you a passage of Scripture to help you in a difficult time, then you know this to be true. Words can wound, but they can also heal.

A Means of Life and a Means of Death

> *Death and life are in the power of the tongue, and those who love it will eat its fruits.*
>
> —Proverbs 18:21

More seriously, the proverbs tell us that words give life, but they can also bring death. The power of our words cannot be overstated. If you are like me and tend to process thoughts verbally, you have to be even more careful, because your words will more often give or take the life of relationships with others in your home. Our words can move people to action or can suffocate them.

There is a story about two frogs that fell into a pit. A group of frogs is bouncing along in the woods. Two of the frogs fall into a pit. The pit is deep, so the other frogs are yelling at these frogs, "You're dead. It's over. Give up." But the frogs at the bottom of the pit both think "If I can just jump high enough, I can get out of this pit." They start jumping over and over. Meanwhile, the frogs on the outside of the pit are yelling, "Give up. It will never work. You can't do it. All hope is lost. Just let yourselves die." One of the frogs listens, quits jumping, and dies. The other frog keeps jumping...higher and higher...and eventually jumps high enough to get out of the pit. The only difference is that the surviving frog was deaf. So, the discouraging words felt to him like words of encouragement. "You can do it! Jump higher!" He survived because he thought they were cheering him on. The moral of the story is that our words can encourage and inspire or they can defeat and destroy.

A Thermometer for the Heart

> *Either make the tree good and its fruit good, or make the tree bad and its fruit bad, for the tree is known by its fruit. You brood of vipers! How can you speak good, when you are evil? For out of the abundance of the heart the mouth speaks. The good person out of his good treasure brings forth good, and the evil person out of his evil treasure brings forth evil.*
> —Matthew 12:33–35

Last, the Bible teaches that words reveal our hearts. When Jesus was on earth, he had to deal with all kinds of different people. The religious leaders proved to be some of the most difficult people Jesus encountered, and Matthew 12 contains an instance where religious leaders see what Jesus is doing and actually begin to spread the lie that his power is demonic. Jesus knows their hearts, and in verse 33 he says something to these people. He explains that the reason they're speaking these harsh, unkind words is that their hearts are wicked. The way we use our words is an issue of our heart.

What Jesus is saying to the religious leaders is true for all of us. Out of the abundance of the heart the mouth speaks, and by our words we are justified or condemned. In time, your heart will be revealed by your words. If your words heal and give life, they reveal a healthy heart. If your words hurt and take life, they reveal a problem in your heart. Our words always reveal our hearts.

When I was an undergraduate at Northeastern State University in Oklahoma, I enjoyed playing intramural sports (where champions are made). My favorite sport was basketball. But something would happen to me when I got on the court. I was so competitive and wanted to win so badly that my speech would totally change. So, off the court I hoped to represent Jesus Christ, but on the basketball court the depths of my heart were revealed. I remember one day in particular when I was approached after the game by an upperclassman—I knew him by his reputation for strong faith in Christ—and after I'd used a series of expletives and talked the kind of trash that would embarrass my mother, he came up to me and said, "Russell, I see you on campus, and I know you're trying to honor God with your life, but when you get on the basketball court, your heart is revealed." And I'll never forget how he quoted this passage to me: "The Bible says that from the overflow of your heart, your mouth will speak."

My first reaction was, "Who are you to tell me how to act?" I was upset because I knew he was right. No matter how hard I'd tried to manage my own mouth, when things got intense a darkness in my heart was revealed through my own words.

Maybe you feel what I felt (and feel) at times; you know you are unable to always control your tongue. "Although we are born with the gift of language, research shows that we are surprisingly unskilled when it comes to communicating with others."[2] Most of us want to create life-giving worlds with our words but fail at times. What do you do? Ask God to transform your heart.

How the Gospel Transforms Our Words

In Ezekiel 36:26, the prophet tells of a time when hearts will be changed. "And I will give you a new heart, and a new spirit I will put within you. And I will remove the heart of stone from your flesh and give you a heart of flesh." Instead of a heart of stone, we need a heart able to respond to God. Here is what God has done in Christ: God has given us new hearts. Maybe you have some behavior you feel unable to overcome or conquer, but you want to stop because you know it destroys you and others. Here's what you must do: ask God to transform your heart. It may not happen overnight, but the start is a heart change which can only be accomplished by God. The Psalmist inspires us to pray, "*Set a guard, O Lord, over my mouth; keep watch over the door of my lips!*" (Psalm 141:3), and "*Let the words of my mouth and the meditation of my heart be acceptable in your sight, O Lord, my rock and my redeemer*" (19:14). We need God to transform our hearts.

All around are messages of how to manage behavior. That might work for a very short period of time, but what we really need is a heart change. You cannot fix the world you have created with your words or change the environment of your home with minor moral adjustments. What you need is a major heart change. A heart change begins to take place whenever we repent of our sins and place our faith in Jesus Christ. This is our declaration that, "I am not perfect. I need Jesus." Go ahead. Say those words out loud. It feels really good. "I am not perfect. I need Jesus." The Bible says that when we confess Jesus as Lord, giving him our lives, the Spirit of God enters our hearts. This begins the needed heart transformation. Then, over time, our behavior will change. The point is, lasting change in how we use our words begins in the heart.

I want to give some really practical things you can do, but if you jump to these practical things without doing the heart work, you are in trouble. You'll try to manage your behavior without first experiencing a genuine heart change. Over time it will just leave you frustrated. Once you've given your life to God through faith in Jesus Christ, there are two ways your behavior will change. You will speak up using your words to create life, and you will stay quiet when needed. I want to focus on how speaking up can create healthy connections.

Speaking Up with Life-Giving Words
Speak up by speaking the truth in love. Remember, words can change the brain. The kind of truth I'm talking about is not self-help truth. Saturday Night Live used to have a character named Stuart Smalley. His well-known

catchphrase was so popular, it became a book: *I'm good enough, I'm smart enough, and doggone it, people like me.* That's not the type of self-talk I'm encouraging. What I'm saying is, speak the truth of Scripture to yourself (and others), and it will change your brain.

Speak up to celebrate the positive more than talking about the negative. Newberg and Waldman have discovered that "the moment a person expresses even the slightest degree of negativity, it increases negativity in both the speaker's and listener's brains."[3] This hinders connection in our homes. In a thought-provoking chapter called "circuit jammers," Wayne Mack writes about ways our speech jams the circuits of communication. One circuit jammer is "excessive negative talk." He writes, "Some people constantly complain and find fault. They seldom affirm or talk about positive virtues of other people ... The gloom and doom that pours from the mouths of these people fosters a depressing atmosphere in the family. Home becomes a place where spirits are weighed down rather than lifted, where heaviness rather than happiness prevails—a place people want to avoid."[4] And, negative speech creates a world that no one really wants to live in. Rather than allowing negativity to jam the communication in our home, we ought to use our words to create a world of celebration! Celebrate the accomplishments of your kids and your spouse.

We have a tradition in our home that happens every time the kids bring home a report card. No matter what their grades are on that card, I ask them, "Did you do your best?" Then, I scoop them up and dance around while spinning and chanting, "Awesome job! I am so proud of you! Woohoo!" (This is one thing that motivates me in the weight room as my kids are getting bigger and harder to pick up!) They love being celebrated, and they are lined up when I get home on report card day to hear my positive words of celebration for them.

The incredible thing about celebration is that over time people will try to become more of what you celebrate. If you praise your children for their good grades, it could inspire them toward better grades. If you praise your children for their kindness to a sibling, they may be even more inclined to be kind. If you celebrate accomplishment, over time your kids will be curious to try new things. Most importantly, if you celebrate the ways you see them reflecting Jesus Christ, it will become their desire to honor God.

Certainly, there is a time to stop the celebrating and instruct children by speaking to their wrong behavior. In fact, that is the best time to teach kids about sin and the need for repentance and faith in Jesus Christ. But, I am convinced it is far more effective to train my children by celebrating the good moments than focusing on the bad. If you're one of those people who tend to talk more about the bad things than the good things, then it's time for a heart change. Go out of your way to celebrate the good things for a week, and just see what happens.

Also, speak up by celebrating your spouse more often. Compliment your spouse privately and in the presence of your children. Our kids ought to see us celebrate each other in the home. Just recently, my wife was away for a night. In the morning, I told my kids, "You know, I really miss your mom." My oldest innocently responded, "Well, she's just been gone a day." I said, "Well, I really miss her because I love her and I love being around her. I miss looking at her beauty and enjoying her great personality!" I'll never forget the look in their eyes as she came home later that day and I celebrated her arrival with my words. Celebrate your spouse in the presence of your kids. It's so powerful to them. When you do, it will set in their minds expectations for how they will want to be treated when looking for a mate.

Speak up when words harm. Certainly, I do have in mind when you notice others using words in a way that creates division in your home. But, I also have in mind when you as a parent are willing to speak up and admit you've spoken in ways that are harsh or unloving. Remember, our aim is that we would live connected to one another in healthy, life-giving relationships so we can be most effective on mission with God in the world. You will not be a perfect parent, so experiencing healthy connections in the home will require you to deal with those moments when you mess up. More often than I'd like to admit, I apologize to my kids and spouse about something I've said that shouldn't have been said in the way I said it or said at all. Most often, I speak harshly when I am tired, rushed, or angry about something that has nothing to do with them. It is a sobering experience to admit error in how I use my words, but I want my kids to know I understand how powerful words can be.

Speak up when necessary. When somebody in your family says something that hurts, talk about it. We are all imperfect, and sometimes we will slip up in the things that we say or do. Not long ago, I accepted an offer to take my kids to a Houston Dynamo soccer game. We didn't get home until 10:00 p.m. One of my sons was way beyond his limit. He had been loaded up with sugary junk food, and his out of control behavior met my tired brain. He tossed a popcorn tub at me, popping me right on the face. He needed to be corrected, but my correction was verbally harsh. We got home and both went to bed without saying another word. As I lay in bed reflecting on how I used my words wrongly, a strong sense of regret came over me. The following morning when I saw him, I said, "I'm sorry. I spoke too harshly to you, and I apologize." He just said, "Can I play games on your phone?" I don't think he heard me, but I felt better just having said it.

The Bible teaches that "no one can tame the tongue" (James 3:8). If you are unable to completely tame your tongue and control the words that come out of your mouth, then what do you do when you mess up? You ask for forgiveness. You humble yourself.

Much of this will be helped if we heed James 1:19: "*Let every person be quick to hear, slow to speak…*" There's a quip that's a little dorky, but it gets to the point: "God gave us two ears and one mouth for a reason." Using our words less often can be a good way of keeping ourselves from having to apologize for the misuse of them.

Our words are so powerful. They will either build connection or sever connection with others in our homes. Fortunately, with our words we can mend relationships that have been harmed by our words. With God's supernatural work in our hearts, our words can strengthen connection so we more fully enjoy one another on mission with him.

Here are some practical ways that I used words to breathe life into my family.

Almost weekly, I call a family meeting. After doing it for some time, when I say the words "family meeting," the kids quickly get together in anticipation of what I am about to announce. Early on it was things like, "We are having another baby!" or, "We are moving!" But more recently I have used these times to remind us all what we are about as a family. A recent speech went something like this: "I love you all so much. You are so special to me and your mom. Each of you has been created by God with special qualities. And, I am proud to be your dad. I have noticed some things recently that I want to celebrate. Koby, you took out the trash without being asked. Keaton, I am so proud of how you are working hard at school. Pryce, your effort in baseball is outstanding. Dryden, you give the best hugs! Way to go! Let's keep loving God and loving others. Also, let's be careful with how we speak to one another. I have noticed some arguing about unimportant things. If you are upset, talk about it calmly. If you can't resolve it alone, ask Mom and me for help. We are a team, and we have to keep working together. One last thing, I just want to remind us all that we believe God gave us this house and put us in this neighborhood to tell our neighbors about Jesus. Let's pray that God will use us here." (To get the real picture, you must imagine the boys flopping around on the couch wrestling while I try to get these words into their heads.)

I have also started doing something really powerful on Valentine's Day. I write a love letter to Jeanie. Then, I call a family meeting. With all the kids listening, I get on one knee and read aloud my letter to Jeanie. It goes something like this: "Jeanie, I adore you. You are the best thing that has ever happened to me. I miss you when I am away at work. I get excited to come home to you. I love the way you work so hard to take care of us all. I know it can be a thankless job, but we would be lost without you. You are beautiful. Your hair, your eyes, your skin, your body, I love it all. I will love you forever." I want my kids to know that the way I speak to their mom is special and sacred.

I write notes to my kids. I don't do it every day, but I try to write notes often and put them in their school lunches. I want them to be surprised with a loving note from me in the middle of their work day. Without exception, they will come home with joy in their eyes that I would take time to use my words to encourage them.

I make time to text people words of encouragement during the day. Often, it is people God puts on my heart. I've found that a simple, "I am thinking about you today. Have a great day!" goes a long way to brighten someone's day. Most often, I text Jeanie with "I am thinking about you," or "I love you," or "Let's put the kids to bed early tonight...if you know what I mean." (With four kids, we have to start planning physical intimacy early in the day. #realtalk) This little effort of using words goes a long way to strengthen the connections with people I love.

These are just a few ways you can use your words to breathe life into your family. Step up and do it. Husbands, speak lovingly to your wife. Wives, affirm your husband. Parents, celebrate your kids while also using your words to give loving instruction. It works. I promise. Connecting your family in mission demands a new way of using your words. Living connected on mission as a family will be wonderful. The words exchanged in your home are a powerful way to strengthen connections so that you can fully engage the mission of God.

Reflection Questions

- Early in the chapter, we looked at four ways that the Bible talks about the effects of our words. Which of these stood out to you the most? Why?

  _____

  _____

  _____

- Have you ever experienced the pain of words that were intended to destroy? How has that experience shaped the trajectory of your life? How has it changed how you view the power of words?

  _____

  _____

  _____

- Read Matthew 12:33–35 again. What does Jesus mean when he talks about being justified or condemned by our words? How does this weighty statement affect your understanding of the Holy Spirit and his work in your heart?

  _____

  _____

  _____

- Your six-year-old child continually lashes out with angry words every time you or your spouse tell him to clean up after himself. What do you need to tell your child about his words? How might the power of your words (by speaking up) be significant in his life?

  _____
  _____
  _____
  _____

- What are three steps you can take to use your words less often—reserving them for meaningful, life-giving opportunities to build up your family for the sake of God's mission in this world?

  _____
  _____
  _____
  _____

CHAPTER 4

Living Connected & Conflict

Conflict will happen. Conflict is a necessary component to living connected in healthy relationships. It is a strange reality, but conflict handled in healthy ways will strengthen relationships beyond what you might imagine is possible. You might want to avoid it, but avoiding conflict will cost you more. Consider an illustration from the marketplace. In the *New York Times* bestselling book *Crucial Conversations,* Joseph Grenny summarizes his research on conflict resolution with a compelling idea. He says employers "save over $1,500 and an eight-hour workday" every time conflict is handled in healthy ways.[1] Mishandled conflict costs something. In business, it costs money. In the home, it costs connection. My hope is to increase your understanding of why conflict happens and how to better handle it so that your family relationships are strengthened. As you learn to better deal with conflict, you will be a healthier family, and you will have an even greater effectiveness serving the Lord as a family on mission.

The Enemy Next Door

What causes conflict? Usually it's just the small things of everyday life done by the people we are around most often. Psychologist Sigmund Freud, in his research entitled "The Narcissism of Minor Differences," helps us understand this by observing that people who live near one another and those who are the most similar are often the ones who have the most intense conflict. He observed people groups: the Spaniards and the Portuguese, the North Germans and the South Germans, the English and the Scotch. These people groups have historically fought most bitterly, but all who lived near one another were culturally quite similar to their enemies. People who are similar, but have small differences, fight the most often.[2] This theory is still used to explain why civil wars happen. But the same is true in our homes. The things that create conflict in our homes are not major differences; they are just little things, annoying things.

I am amazed, really, at how often parenting is helping my children resolve conflict between each other.

Just this morning, I was awakened by conflict in my home.

6-year-old: (at my bedside crying) Someone ate my blue peeps*!

*squishy, sugar-covered, marshmallow Easter bunny-shaped peeps

Me: How do you know someone ate your blue peeps? Did you eat them?

6-year-old: (on floor crying) I only ate two! Or three... maybe four.

Me: (calls children together...rolls eyes) Who ate his blue peeps?

13-year-old: Oh. I thought those were my blue peeps. Wait, I had yellow peeps.

6-year-old: (hotter than 1,000 suns) Why did you eat my blue peeps? Those were my blue peeps*! I hate you! (launches at 13 year old arms flailing)

*at this point, I hope to never hear the word "peeps" again

Me: You made a mistake. Do the right thing. Give him your yellow peeps. Conflict solved.

Clearly, I am a master of conflict resolution. But, the hope is that by the time the six-year-old becomes an adult, he can better handle this situation without my intervention.

Aggression and Passivity: Our Unhealthy Defaults

The unfortunate reality is that many adults have never been taught how to deal with conflict in healthy ways. Without instruction and God's help, most people deal with conflict by one of two extremes: aggression or passivity.

One of the most difficult counseling cases I've dealt with began when a couple, Josh and Sara, walked into my office with divorce papers in hand. I asked them to meet with me as a last attempt to save their marriage. Surprisingly, they began the conversation very calmly. They shared their story of how they met in college, quickly fell in love, and enjoyed a very happy first few months of marriage. Things became difficult when Josh started traveling more for work. It was especially hard because Josh had moved Sara away from her family, who provided a strong support to her. Sara was alone; Josh was busy. Then, the conflict began. It started with little things like Josh leaving his dirty clothes on the floor. Then, it escalated when Sara spent more money than Josh thought was necessary on clothes. These are normal things for a young couple to have conflict over, but the way they fought was very unhealthy. Josh would become aggressive (much like he saw his father talk to his mom). Sara would hide in another room (much like she learned to adapt when conflict arose in her childhood home). Josh would get more aggressive. Sara would more often disappear.

Every part of their relationship suffered. They talked less. The trust between them diminished, which affected their physical intimacy. Of course, they still had natural desire to connect intimately with another person, so each of them had begun sexual relationships with other people. It was a mess that all began with their inability to handle normal conflict in healthy ways. Over the course of several months, I met with them and offered the most basic of ideas and biblical teachings, providing them the tools to heal and rebuild their marriage in a healthier way. It has been truly difficult for them as they continue to build trust and deal with conflict in a way that enables them to live connected on mission. I remain hopeful for Josh and Sara.

Live at Peace

Appropriately handling conflict is critical to living connected. Without it, there will never be peace in the home, and a peaceful home reflects the work of God in the world. This is why peace is held as such a high ideal in Scripture.

In Romans 12:18 NIV, Paul tells the Roman believers as they are establishing their new church, *"If it is possible, as far as it depends on you, live at peace with everyone."* Later in the letter, Paul urges, *"Let us therefore make every effort to do what leads to peace and to mutual edification"* (Rom. 14:19 NIV)." Paul writes to the fledgling church in Ephesus, in Ephesians 4:3 NIV: *"Make every effort to keep the unity of the Spirit through the bond of peace."* Another passage to set the stage for this conversation on conflict is Hebrews 12:14 NIV: *"Make every effort to live in peace with all men and to be holy; without holiness no one will see the Lord."*

Here is the aim: families experiencing a peaceful home with connected individuals who can deal with conflict in healthy ways. This enables a family to live connected on mission.

Why We Don't Live at Peace

Where did the trouble begin?

The story of Cain and Abel, the first children of Adam and Eve, results in a murder of one by the other. You might remember, Genesis chapters 1 and 2 tell the story of God creating the world. In Genesis 3, Adam and Eve rebel against God; they disobey God and sin enters the world, creating division. In chapter 4, we begin to see the impact of sin on relationships. It is striking to learn that the first biblical story about a family results in murder. It seems like God wants us to see something here: that in the very beginning of time, in the first human interactions, conflict was a result of the division caused by sin. This passage can teach us about conflict and how it affects our families.

¹Now Adam knew Eve his wife, and she conceived and bore Cain, saying, "I have gotten a man with the help of the Lord." ²And again, she bore his brother Abel. Now Abel was a keeper of sheep, and Cain a worker of the ground. ³In the course of time Cain brought to the Lord an offering of the fruit of the ground, ⁴and Abel also brought of the firstborn of his flock and of their fat portions. And the Lord had regard for Abel and his offering, ⁵but for Cain and his offering he had no regard. So Cain was very angry, and his face fell. ⁶The Lord said to Cain, "Why are you angry, and why has your face fallen? ⁷If you do well, will you not be accepted? And if you do not do well, sin is crouching at the door. Its desire is contrary to you, but you must rule over it."

⁸Cain spoke to Abel his brother. And when they were in the field, Cain rose up against his brother Abel and killed him. ⁹Then the Lord said to Cain, "Where is Abel your brother?" He said, "I do not know; am I my brother's keeper?" ¹⁰And the Lord said, "What have you done? The voice of your brother's blood is crying to me from the ground. ¹¹And now you are cursed from the ground, which has opened its mouth to receive your brother's blood from your hand. ¹²When you work the ground, it shall no longer yield to you its strength. You shall be a fugitive and a wanderer on the earth." ¹³Cain said to the Lord, "My punishment is greater than I can bear. ¹⁴Behold, you have driven me today away

from the ground, and from your face I shall be hidden. I shall be a fugitive and a wanderer on the earth, and whoever finds me will kill me." ^{15}*Then the Lord said to him, "Not so! If anyone kills Cain, vengeance shall be taken on him sevenfold." And the Lord put a mark on Cain, lest any who found him should attack him.* ^{16}*Then Cain went away from the presence of the Lord and settled in the land of Nod, east of Eden.*

Genesis 4:1–16

Adam and Eve obeyed God's command to be fruitful and multiply, and Eve gave birth to Cain and Abel. Abel was the keeper of sheep, and Cain was a worker of the ground. Abel worked with animals, while Cain grew plants. They were both working to bring to God an offering. Abel brings an animal, sacrifices it, and offers it to God. Cain brings a grain offering and offers it to God. God accepts Abel's sacrifice as good, but he rejects Cain's sacrifice.

Scholars debate about why God accepted Abel's and not Cain's. Some believe it was because Abel brought an animal sacrifice, which involved the shedding of blood, and it pointed to Jesus's shed blood being an acceptable sacrifice. This is a possible explanation, but more obvious is that God accepted Abel's because of the heart with which he made the sacrifice. In contrast, Cain's heart was not right. This is why Abel's offering was considered better by God (Hebrews 11:4). Abel's offering was brought to God by faith, with a sincere heart toward God. God counted him righteous and accepted it. Cain's offering was not accepted. It was not as much about the actual sacrifice as it was about the heart with which it was brought before God. We see Cain's heart exposed when he gets angry enough to murder his own brother. Abel's heart was right. Cain's heart was not right.

What goes on between Cain and Abel reveals something about the human heart that can result in conflict, as well as the kind of behavior that would lead somebody like Cain to murder his brother Abel.

Take Responsibility

After Cain murders his brother, God comes to him and says, "Hey, where's your brother?" God gives Cain an opportunity to admit that his heart is wicked and that he has murdered his brother. Cain essentially responds, "Who am I? Am I my brother's keeper?" (Genesis 4:9). He deflects his responsibility for where his brother has gone, even though Abel is gone (literally) as a result of a conflict with Cain.

An interesting thing happens when there is conflict in our homes: we tend to shift the responsibility and blame another person. We want to say, "Something may have happened, but I don't want to be responsible for it; it's not my job to keep up with somebody else; it's not my job to consider how I may be responsible for the harm done in this relationship."

Recently, this played out in my own home. It was an especially stressful week for me at work with a few sleepless nights. As the days passed, I got home tired and more agitated. On Friday, I walked into what felt like a messy, chaotic home. Shortly after walking in the door, I barked at the kids about leaving the house such a mess. Then, I turned to Jeanie and asked, "So, what did you do today?" Innocent, right? No way, and she knew what I meant by asking it. I was really asking, "What Netflix shows have you watched while lounging around instead of cleaning this house so that when I get home, AFTER A LONG, STRESSFUL, HARD WEEK, I can walk into a peaceful, orderly home?"

Let the conflict begin. In our home, I get aggressive. Jeanie gets quiet. Well, she used to get quiet. She is now finding her voice when we have conflict, and I wasn't going to get away with such a poorly timed attempt at rebuking her for the house being such a mess. After letting me vent about how others are ultimately the source of my irritation (i.e., passing the responsibility for the source of conflict), she quietly lifted her finger to point to the piles of my things adding to the mess. A sock. A pair of shoes. An unpacked suitcase from a trip I'd taken. Then, she softly began listing what she had been doing all day. She spent extra time with our oldest on a school project. She had gone to the grocery store. She had taken our youngest to the doctor for his annual check-up. And, she spent time arranging for a babysitter so she could surprise me with a date night. Yep, I am a jerk. I started the conflict. Then, I wanted to pass responsibility for the problem off on others. In the end, the responsibility was all mine. My heart was not right. No, that's too soft. The wickedness that remains in my heart was exposed. Just like Cain. It's much easier to identify sin in others' lives, but our primary responsibility is not for the sin of others. (Let that sink in. Reread it. Admit it. It's true.)

I want to love my wife as long as I live. I want to be seventy-five years old with a bunch of kids—at least four—and a bunch of grandkids, and I want to look over at my wife and love her deeply. Even at seventy-five years old, I want my heart to burn with passion and desire for my wife. How is that going to be possible? We have to learn to connect deeply now. This requires us to think about resolving normal conflicts in our home and committing to work through differences.

You must own your responsibility. That is part of growing and developing emotional maturity. When you experience conflict, ask yourself, "Self, is there something you've done to cause or add to this conflict?" More often than not, we can take part of the responsibility for whatever is causing the difficulty.

Identify the Root

Once we acknowledge responsibility, we must get to the root of the issue. All conflict is a result of a deeper issue, and that issue is sin. Left alone, the sin will hinder connection with others. Sin is the part of us that's not yet made whole and right before God, the part in us that tends to rebel against God. The location of that sin is deep in our hearts.

Imagine coming to your pastor's office because you were fighting with your spouse.

Scenario #1:

You: "My wife and I are in a huge fight."
Pastor: "Just stay away until things settle down. Let her work out her own issues."
You: "So, just let things blow over?"

Pastor: "Yes, then just don't make her mad again."

You walk out the door without the pastor talking about issues related to your own heart. Ugh! The situation might defuse, but it will come up again. Why? Because, the pastor has not led you on the difficult journey to examine your own heart for areas of sin that create conflict in your home. All conflict results from sin in the heart. (Note: Find a new church.)

Scenario #2:
You: "My wife and I are in a huge fight."
Pastor: "Why? What in your heart is adding to the conflict?"
You: "Huh?" (This is the response I typically get when I press into the heart issues. It is complex and requires a lot of courage to honestly assess what is in our hearts.)
Pastor: "All conflict results from sin. What sinful attitudes result in actions that are your responsibility in this conflict?"
You: "I have a quick temper. There is anger in my heart."
Pastor: "Only God can change your heart. Put your trust in him to transform your heart through the power of the gospel."

In Cain's heart, the sin is difficult to identify (it was something related to him not offering his sacrifice with sincerity of faith). But, it manifested itself in anger (I have discussed anger in chapter 2). His anger gave way to rage, leading to murder. We are all tempted, like Cain, to ignore the real issues that result in conflict. James 4:1–2 says, *"What causes quarrels and fights among you? Is it not this, that your passions are at war within you?"* There's something deep within you that causes the quarrels and fights. The heart is the place we must first go to do work.

Once the sin begins to be seen, only one power can change our hearts. It's the Spirit of God working to do something for us that we could never do for ourselves; that is, the Spirit of God exposes those sin areas and transforms them so we can become more like Jesus Christ. This is why we need Jesus. Through faith in Jesus we receive the Holy Spirit of God who begins working on us. God's Spirit working supernaturally in us is able to root out the sin in our hearts so we can become more like Christ in how we handle conflict.

If you have never received Christ through faith, you can try to manage your behavior. And it might work for a little while, but ultimately it will never change your heart. For us to experience the kinds of relationships God designed us to experience, the deepest parts of our hearts must change.

The only way they will change is by the gospel working in our hearts. I would be negligent to give you practical actions to make your relationships better at home without first telling you the gospel of Jesus Christ. If you start with the practice of trying to manage your behavior before dealing with sin in your heart, you are in trouble.

Discover the Ripple Effects

Once we take responsibility for our part and begin identifying the sin in our own hearts, we then better understand how our behavior affects others. After murdering his brother, Cain's unaddressed sin affected many generations. In fact, Cain and his descendants represent evil in the entire Old Testament narrative. It's true, the way we deal with conflict affects others. Most of all, children are affected by how parents handle conflict. Just like Cain's pattern of conflict affected his kids, my patterns of conflict will affect my kids (just as my parents shaped my patterns). Again, it goes back to the impact made by our family of origin.

How do you handle conflict? How did you observe your parents deal with conflict? Did you see your parents fight? How did they fight? Was there screaming? Was there hitting? Did one or both stomp out of the room avoiding the conflict altogether? Or, did you observe your parents handle disagreement in healthy ways? In looking back, did they aim for peace in the home and appropriately handle difficulties as they arose? The answers to these kinds of questions are the greatest factor in your own way of dealing with conflict. All of us can recall ways our parents dealt with conflict. Some of it was not good. I hope that some of it for you was helpful in preparing you for adulthood.

I mentioned to you earlier that I tend to deal with conflict by becoming loud or assertive (okay, aggressive). Jeanie tends to hide. I call it the "roly poly" conflict style. (You know, those little bugs that curl up in a ball when you poke at them?) She hates conflict. So, when we were first married, I would thunder. Jeanie would hide in an attempt to weather the storm. It was not healthy, but we didn't know any different. You see, I learned to deal with conflict from my family of origin. For complex reasons, I learned that to be heard I needed to become the loudest voice in the room. And, Jeanie grew up in a home where there was little to no conflict. I mean, really, conflict was avoided even when it is obviously needed to deal with issues. So, we got married, along with our family of origin issues, and we begin to have our own family. We now have four children (the oldest of whom is a teenager) and I can already see how our ways of handling conflict are impacting our children. One of them becomes the loudest in the room when conflict arises. Another is great at deflecting the main issue in hopes of avoiding responsibility. Still another is so freaked out when anyone gets into even the smallest of arguments that he immediately gets emotional. What have I done? In just a few short years, I have already failed at raising kids who can perfectly handle conflict. So, I need help. And you do, too!

For those who have faith in Christ and have begun the hard work of assessing our own hearts, can we just admit that conflict is normal? If I am doing a premarital counseling session and the couple cannot think of a time when they ever had conflict, I am concerned. Why? Because it reveals that the couple is not connecting like they ought to be. Every relationship that can be described as close eventually experiences some type of conflict. It doesn't mean it always results in arguing, but it does mean that something will happen that requires both people to exercise some conflict resolution skills.

If you are struggling to deal with conflict, it will be difficult for you to be about the mission of God in the world. It is difficult because your focus will be on the unresolved problems in your relationships. You might be inspired by the idea, "God wants to use your life to impact the world." You see the fires in the city around you. You believe God can use you in those places to bring hope and healing. But, you cannot even begin to think about how to do it because you have fires to put out in your own relationships.

Can you imagine a family not mired in conflict? Can you imagine your family connected on mission? The truth of the matter is that a family can use the heat of conflict in the home to grow stronger. Although conflict is normal, allowing unresolved conflict to exist in your relationships does not have to become normal.

Dealing with conflict by becoming overly aggressive or strangely absent is not the way to live connected on mission. I think of the way of Jesus Christ, who was neither passive by ignoring our sin or aggressive by destroying us in our sin. Instead, he stepped into the conflict caused by our sin to bring reconciliation in a loving way.

Starting Point for Handling Conflict

Your responsibility in appropriately handling conflict in your home is first and foremost to tune into God. That's where it starts. When there is conflict in your home, don't immediately go to battle. The first thing you need to do is get on your knees and say, "God help me to see things that I cannot see. Help me to discover in my own heart the sin that is contributing to this conflict. Is it jealousy? Is it pride? Is it a desire to control everything? What is it? Is it fear? Help me, God." This is how you care for your responsibility in your home. First you must go to God, and that requires you to turn in faith to Jesus for a relationship with God.

A. W. Tozer, in his book *The Pursuit of God*, gives this illustration. He asks the question, "Has it ever occurred to you that 1,000 pianos all tuned to the same fork are automatically tuned to each other? They are of one accord." They are not tuned to each other, but they are tuned to one standard, so they all sound the same.[3] Imagine in your home when there's conflict if all parties involved got tuned to the Father. Imagine what the result would be. You'd be tuned to one another. Rather than first going to one another to have the battle, we must first tune to God.

Be someone who's passionate about peace in your home. This requires you to know that some conflict is normal. It requires you to know your story. It requires you to take on your responsibility. Be in tune to God, first and foremost. It requires you to pursue peace and to extend grace. If you do these things, I believe you'll be on the path to experiencing the kind of family that God will use on mission.

Reflection Questions

- What is the "Narcissism of Minor Differences," and how does this observation affect how you view conflict in your home?

_____
_____
_____
_____

- Do you tend toward aggression or passivity? What's one recent example of how your tendency to one of these has affected your family?

- What heart motives and drives are at the root of how you've been handling conflict at home recently?

- How have you seen your poor handling of conflict ripple beyond what you originally anticipated?

- List three ways you need to tune your heart to God in preparation for the coming conflicts in your home.

CHAPTER 5

Living Connected & Touch

It is about to get uncomfortable. I want to help you understand the power of touch to build connection in your home. Now, hear me out. This is not going to be creepy, but I want you to recognize what can be a missed opportunity to build meaningful connections. One of the more important, least talked about ways to strengthen connection in our homes is by how we use physical touch to express love to one another. My guess is that you have not ever heard a sermon or read a book that helped you think about how powerful physical touch can be. In our society, sexuality and physical touch have been so corrupted that we're nervous people will immediately think dirty thoughts. What God intends for good, the enemy tries to distort and use for evil. For many people, physical touch to bond with others in our home does not happen as naturally as it could (or should). We have to work on it by being intentional and thoughtful in how we use touch in healthy ways. Keep in mind what we are aiming for. We want our families to connect in healthy ways so we can walk together on mission. The Bible demonstrates how powerful touch can be.

Science and the Power of Touch

To begin making progress in the right direction, we need to take a look at some impressive conclusions being developed by scientists and psychologists. Substantial research over the past decade on the science of touch is proving what we know intuitively to be true: our sense of touch directly influences our sense of ourselves. David Linden, an expert in the science of touch, states that "our entire skin is a sensing, guessing, logic-seeking organ of perception, a blanket with a brain in every micro-inch."[1] Said another way, the way we feel in our hearts is impacted greatly by what we feel physically. I love how one writer puts it: "We see our skins as hides hung around our inner life, when, in so many ways, they *are* the inner life, pushed outside."[2]

Another thought-provoking study was done by a leading psychologist, Dacher Keltner. He co-authored one influential study that encoded twelve distinct kinds of "celebratory touches" among pro basketball players, including "fist bumps, high-fives, chest bumps, leaping shoulder bumps, chest punches, head slaps, head grabs, low fives, high tens, full hugs, half hugs, and team huddles." He discovered that teams whose players touched one another a lot did better than those whose players didn't. Touch lowers stress, builds morale, and produces triumphs—a chest bump instructs us in cooperation, a half hug in compassion.[3]

Another researcher noted:

> Our bodies have eighteen square feet of skin, which makes skin our largest organ. Because skin cannot shut its eyes or cover its ears, it is on a constant state of readiness to receive messages—it is always on. The first sensory input in life comes from the sense of touch while still in the womb, and touch continues to be the primary means of experiencing the world throughout infancy and well into childhood, even into aging.[4]

Touch can be any form of physical contact that stirs in the other person feelings of being loved. According to biologists, affectionate touch releases a hormone called oxytocin that makes us feel good about the person who touches us. Whenever you touch someone, or someone touches you in a healthy, affectionate way, your body releases hormones telling your brain that the person is kind and loving. Healthy physical touch to express feelings of affection is critical in our homes.

In the book *Forever and Always: The Art of Intimacy,* Steven and Celestia Tracy discuss our culture of excess—that so many people have so much extra—but when it comes to affectionate touch, one of the most essential commodities in life, we are some of the most impoverished people in the world. Americans, particularly American youth, are being touch-starved and are paying a significant price for this deprivation.[5] Listen carefully: healthy physical touch is one of the most misused, neglected tools in the home for building healthy connections.

Healthy physical affection in our homes can also be a powerful agent of healing. In a study done to discover the power of physical touch, scientists observed a group of nurses, caregivers, and massage therapists. They found that the power of physical affection was enough to reduce blood pressure, pain, and nausea by as much as fifty percent among the patients.[6] Another study also revealed that physical affection was able to stimulate premature newborns to gain forty-seven percent more weight, and physical affection was able to significantly boost the immune system of HIV positive adults.[7]

With the weight of the scientific community behind us, we can confidently say that touch is powerful. You have in your hands, with loving touch, the power to connect with others in your home.

The Bible and the Power of Touch

You might be surprised how often the Bible models touch as a natural way to express love. There are many verses that talk about how important, beautiful, and worthy of celebration physical touch is between a husband and wife and between family members.

The Power of Touch for Your Spouse

To start, did you know the Bible talks with intimate detail about the importance of healthy physical touch between husband and wife? For an eye-opening look into ways that a married couple expresses love through touching, read Song of Solomon. It might surprise you. Solomon's bride is getting warmed up in 1:2; the bride says of her husband, "*Let him kiss me with the kisses of his mouth! For your love is better than wine."* She is expressing the desire of every wife, and that is to be kissed (touched) in healthy, loving ways. Her desire for his touch results from her awareness of how much he loves her. His love for her is better than something she already really enjoys (the taste of wine). So, she wants him to kiss her. It is a good thing when your spouse wants a kiss. Am I right? Learning to touch our spouse to express love in healthy ways is so important for connection.[8]

The Power of Touch for Your Children
The Bible also normalizes physical touch between parents and children.

In Genesis 27, we read about an unfortunate incident when Jacob steals his older brother Esau's birthright and blessing. Within the story, there's a moment when Isaac, the father, greets his son, saying, "Come near and kiss me, my son." This may feel odd to our American way, because rarely would you see an older adult male kiss his adult male son. We now live in a culture where men are seemingly less capable of vulnerable expressions of physical affection. Steven and Celestia Tracy point out that "many men have come to feel tentative or even insecure in their masculinity, so they bolster their sense of masculinity by tenaciously avoiding or denying what they perceive as feminine qualities such as physical expressions of love, acknowledging weaknesses, or any relational experience of vulnerability."[9] And, men tend to easily dismiss the need for physical touch from family members with phrases like, "I'm just not a touchy-feely person." Okay, I get it. Not everyone is as much a "touchy-feely" person as another might be, but we cannot dismiss the proven need our spouse and children have for us to express love through touch in healthy ways. In many different places in the Bible, a parent will kiss a child and a child will kiss a parent as a sign of affection and of connection. Physical affection is normal. It's healthy.

The Power of Touch in Conveying Blessing

We also see places in the Bible where a kiss and a show of affection in the home are a blessing. More than just physically demonstrating what you feel in your heart toward one another, the kiss is actually a blessing. It's a way of encouraging peace and goodness on the person to whom you're expressing your affection. For example, Genesis 31:55 says, *"Early in the morning Laban arose and kissed his grandchildren and his daughters and blessed them. Then Laban departed and returned home."* We'll see later that Jesus does this same thing.

The Power of Touch in Restoring Relationships

We also see physical affection in the story of Joseph in Genesis 45. Before this chapter, Joseph's brothers had sold him into slavery because they were jealous of him. He suffered a long time, but eventually worked his way up and became a powerful person in a foreign land. Finally, after many years, Joseph's brothers come to him in need, not even recognizing him. But instead of cursing or killing them for the way they treated him, Joseph is able to bless them and show them grace.

Genesis 45 shows the reunion between Benjamin and Joseph. Benjamin's other brothers were the ones responsible for sending Joseph into slavery, but Benjamin was Joseph's closest brother and had not known his brothers sold Joseph. When Benjamin and Joseph recognize each other, there was a great reunion: *"Then [Joseph] fell upon his brother Benjamin's neck and wept, and Benjamin wept upon his neck"* (Genesis 45:14–15). After that, he kissed all of his brothers and wept upon them.

It's interesting to notice in the Bible how normal physical touch is when people are reunited after a period separation. The separation might be because of travel, or it could even be caused by conflict. Think about the power of physical affection in a reunion after a period of strife, fighting, and conflict. Have you ever experienced that in your family? Have you experienced separation because of conflict, and then once you are reunited all you wanted to do was embrace the person with whom you've been in conflict? We also see these patterns of affection in the Bible. When two people are reunited after a period of separation, they usually hug and kiss.

There are many other examples of godly, healthy individuals in the Bible who expressed love through physical touch.

- Joseph held his father closely "a good while" (Gen. 46:29)
- David hugged and kissed a friend who was like his brother (1 Sam. 20:41)
- Two sisters, Ruth and Orpah, expressed love in a kiss and hug to their mother-in-law Naomi (Ruth 1:14)
- Paul was hugged and kissed by the elders in Ephesus prior to departing (Acts 20:36–38)
- The prodigal son was greeted by his father with an embrace and kiss (Luke 15:20)

Jesus and the Power of Touch

The most compelling case for this idea of physical touch being a normal way of expressing love to strengthen connection is in the life of Jesus Christ. More than once, Jesus spoke words of truth that were accompanied by physically touching the person. It was his most powerful combination for him to teach people about his mission.

The Touch of Jesus Gives Significance to the Insignificant
In Matthew 19 Jesus is busy teaching large crowds. After addressing a hotly debated issue regarding divorce, some parents from the crowd began bringing children to Jesus for prayer. They hoped he would lay his hands on them to bless them. It's interesting to note that the laying on of hands (i.e., touch) was also done for healing (Mark 6:5, Luke 4:40, Acts 9, and other verses), for reception of the Holy Spirit (Acts 8:17–19), and for ordination (e.g., Acts 6:6, 13:3). So, the "laying on of hands" was a special touch that gave an even greater expression to the words spoken. The combination of words and touch is an incredibly powerful way to communicate love.

Children in this day were socially powerless and dependent. The disciples behaved like most other adults would have in their attempt to keep the children from coming near Jesus. But, Jesus is teaching them about what the Kingdom of God is like; that is, even little children find their place as valued citizens in the Kingdom of God. Jesus says, "Let the little children come to me and do not hinder them, for to such belongs the kingdom of heaven" (Matthew 19:14). He could have easily just spoken words over them, but he chooses a more affectionate way. Matthew says, "He laid his hands on them and went away" (19:15). Mark 10:16 gives even greater detail of his loving touch: *"And he took them in his arms and blessed them, laying his hands on them."* It is his way of saying, "I love you. You are blessed." To Jesus, touch was a powerful way of communicating acceptance and love.

The Touch of Jesus Gives Healing to the Hurting
Not only did Jesus demonstrate that touch is a powerful way of showing love to children, but by his touch he most often heals the sick. This is especially powerful if you consider that Jesus had the power in his words alone to do supernatural work (think: cast out demons or calm the storms). So it is reasonable to say that his touch to heal was his way of communicating a special kind of love. In Matthew 20, Jesus heals with his touch. As Jesus and his disciples are leaving Jericho, a large crowd followed him. Two blind men were sitting by the roadside, and when they heard Jesus going by, they shouted, "Lord, have mercy on us, Son of David!" The crowd rebuked them and told them to be quiet, but they shouted all the louder. "Lord, have mercy on us, Son of David!"

Jesus stopped and called to them, "What do you want me to do for you?" "Lord," they answered, "we want our sight." Jesus had compassion on them and touched their eyes. He could have easily kept walking and spoken words of healing, but Jesus knows about the power of touch to show love. So, he took the time then to touch their eyes, which brought healing. Not only does science give evidence that physical touch has the power to heal, but Jesus chose touch as a tool to heal.

How the Gospel Transforms How We Touch

Scripture teaches us how normal expressing love through physical touch can be. But, you might still feel awkward about it. Maybe you grew up in a home where you cannot remember being hugged or kissed in a healthy way. I don't want to minimize the reality that some people grow up in homes with serious dysfunction in this area. I pray you are encouraged by what I am saying, not ashamed or embarrassed by it. It is not my purpose to deal in detail with all the ways that touch can be used inappropriately in the home; instead, I want to raise awareness that touch to express love is one of the most effective ways to strengthen connections.

If it feels difficult to express your love more often for your spouse and kids with healthy physical touch, then there may a deeper heart issue that needs to be addressed. Sure, not everyone is going to be as physically affectionate as another, but the power of touch to build connection cannot be overstated. As with any heart issue, we must ask, "Does God need to do something in my heart that I cannot do myself?"

The Gospel Enables Genuine Love

At the risk of oversimplifying what needs to happen in our hearts, let me remind you of the two greatest commandments: "Love God. Love Others." It is possible that what all of us need to be more able to connect with those in our homes is to grow in love. Herein is the heart change needed in all of us. But, we cannot do this on our own. We need the supernatural work of God in our hearts to make us more loving people.

In 1 John 4:19, we read, "We love because God first loved us." Hence, our love for others is directly influenced by our understanding of God's love for us. For some, the reason we hold back healthy physical touch is that we lack a sincere love for our spouse or children. It is like our love has a glass ceiling that hinders connection. The result is a physical distancing from our spouse and children.

The Gospel Brings Our Hearts to Life

Our love for others will grow as our hearts are impacted by the love of God. We most clearly see the love of God at the cross. Listen to Paul describe the love of God for you: *"But God, being rich in mercy, because of the great love with which he loved us, even when we were dead in our trespasses, made us alive together with Christ—by grace you have been saved"* (Ephesians 2:4–5).

Sit back and let this soak into your heart. Apart from the love of God through Jesus Christ, you are spiritually dead, foolishly following the devil along the course of this world (Ephesians 2:1–2). Apart from the love of God through Jesus Christ, you are living by the passions of your flesh, deserving the wrath of God (Ephesians 2:3). It may be hard to stomach, but it is the truth. Dead. Distant. Decadent. This is your life without God.

"But God."

I cannot think of a place in the Bible with a more abrupt turn. These two words, "But God" mean so much. We deserve the wrath of God, but God. We were spiritually dead, but God. God is merciful, choosing to give us love rather than wrath. God became flesh to touch humanity with His love. His loving touch through Christ makes us alive. If you will believe that God loves you enough to become flesh so your heart can be raised from the dead to a new life in Christ, then you are saved!

Genuine Love + Living Heart = Powerful Touch

The degree to which we are gripped by this amazing love is the greatest factor in how we are able to love others. Period. And, as our love for others intensifies, so will our natural expression of love through healthy physical touch. It's quite simple, the people we love the most get our most intimate expressions of love by physical touch. I love my wife more than anyone on this earth. The way I touch her is an expression of that love. I love my kids. I hug them and hold them in a way that expresses my love for them in ways that words never could. I have friends I genuinely love. I hug them to express that love. But I don't touch everyone, because I don't love everyone in the same way.

Applying the Power of Touch to Your Home

As you start to understand the love of God for you in Christ, and you desire to demonstrate that love to those around you, you might say, "Okay, but what practical actions can I take?" Let me give you some practical ways to demonstrate love with physical touch.

Kiss Your Spouse Every Day

Apparently, there is actual scientific study on kissing. It is called "philematology." Google it. The research reveals that kissing has many health benefits, including that it reduces stress, increases happiness, and burns calories.[10] And, it's just plain fun! I heard recently about a sermon where the preacher challenged his married congregants to kiss their spouse for 21 seconds at least once a day for 21 days. At first, I thought, "that sounds fun!" Then, I was struck by the realization that it was difficult to find 21 seconds in a day to stop and kiss my own wife. Now, I know there are some newlyweds reading this book that find this hard to believe. But, it's true. Over time, we get so busy with kids, work, and life, that taking the time to express this simple expression of love with our spouse feels nearly impossible. And, the cost is the strength of connection in our marriages. So, I pass on that pastor's challenge to you. Kiss your spouse for 21 seconds each day for 21 days. Set an alarm on your phone to remind you and time you. And, if you are smart, you will schedule those 21 seconds at a time when you have more free time afterward, just in case it stirs in each of you a desire to express yourself in more intimate physical ways. (You are welcome.)[11]

Talk about Touch

Another practical step is to have a serious conversation with your spouse and ask this question: Are your needs for affection being met? Here's what's likely. Some of you are so busy, you don't know that the other person's need for love expressed by touch is not being met. You'd be surprised.

A man told me this week that his wife has left him after quite a few years. When he found out that she was feeling distant from him, he was shocked. He had no clue.

There were a number of years in which her needs were not being met, and her heart began to drift. Eventually, they found themselves in the situation where she was no longer interested in being committed to him.

Have a conversation with your spouse. It's very simple. Ask this: Do you feel like I love you in the way that I touch you? Some men touch their wives in a way that stems from insecurity, in a way that is sophomoric or immature, because they are trying to guard themselves in case of rejection. You must take time for this important conversation. Are your needs being met? Do you feel like I love you in the way I touch you? Or do you feel used? Honest conversations like this can build trust, and trust is an essential ingredient for connection that is strengthened by healthy physical touch.

Hold Your Kids

At the start of each day, hold your kids. Depending on when they awaken and you have to leave for work, this may be impossible to do every day. If they are younger, take one minute most mornings and let them jump into your lap as they are waking up for the day. I find that these slow moments of letting my young children awaken while sitting with me helps them feel loved and helps me more calmly begin what is always a busy day. As they get older, a simple hug will mean the world to them. I realize that teenagers get weird, but I believe in every teenager is still a little child who wants to be reminded they are loved unconditionally. A hug goes a long way! Here is the reality: the frequency and quality with which we show physical affection to our kids will directly impact how they express themselves with touch as adults.[12] And, because your kids are hard-wired to experience love through healthy physical touch, neglecting to show affection to them in this way will leave them touch-starved. If it's awkward for you, take some simple steps to make some changes in how you express love to your kids through physical touch. I promise, the benefit for their souls will exceed the cost to your sense of comfort. At the very least, hug your kids every day.

Balance Discipline with Affection
All parents are trying to sort out how to best discipline our kids. I am learning that sometimes misbehavior is the way that they communicate a need not being met. Touch is a powerful way that we as parents can communicate love in the midst of needing to correct. On occasion, rather than disciplining kids in the way they would expect, gently embrace your child. There have been times when my kids have lost themselves emotionally and become out of control. Rather than disciplining them by setting them away from the family (i.e., time out), I'll wrap them up and hold them tight, squeezing them until they know there's nothing in the world that will separate them from me— that I love them. Admittedly, this doesn't always work, but there have been times when a child has just melted in my arms and calmed down with this physical expression of love.

Wrestle with Your Kids
There is something within every kid (especially boys) that makes them want to test their physical strength on Dad. I have seen it in my own home with three rowdy,

rambunctious boys. All I have to do is say, "Hey, let's do this." When I say those words, they know they are about to get loved on in a very manly way with soft punches and frequent tickles. Sure, there are times when I'll just sit next to my boys or even snuggle with them in the bed while watching sports, but the healthy physical touch that comes from rolling around on the floor can really build connection. Although my wife loves playing with our sons, we have learned it is less natural for her to be rough with the boys in the same way I am. If they are allowed to be too rough with her and treat her carelessly or disrespectfully, then this sets in them an expectation of what their future spouses will allow. We are teaching them that there is a natural way to be physical as an expression of love, but not every person gets the same kind of physical affection.

Kiss Your Kids

Daughters especially resonate with an appropriate kiss. As my daughter grows older. I am increasingly aware of the reality that someday she will live at another man's house. She will be married. (Sigh.) I literally tear up at the thought of giving her away to another man. I think often of this reality. And, I consider it a sacred privilege to do my part in helping her become a fully functioning adult and (if God wills) wife. One critical role I have in her life is to teach her that it is God's design for love to be expressed through physical touch. When I kiss her on the cheek or head multiple times a day as an expression of my love for her, I know it is setting in her the expectation of how her future husband will express love to her. Someday, she will love a man more deeply and in different ways than she is able to love me. Then, she will give and receive love in more intimate ways. The same is true of how my wife expresses loving affection to my sons. She kisses them often.

Celebrate Reunion with Touch
In the evening, develop a pattern of celebrating reunion with physical touch. Every evening when I get home from work, we use physical touch to celebrate the reunion after a day away. Jeanie has been busy managing our home and running errands. The kids have been busy at school and after school activities. I have been away at work. This busy reality of our lives could lead to disconnect in our home. In fact, it has at times. We are trying to lessen these times that busyness keeps us from connecting in healthy ways by these little physical affection reunions each evening just before dinner. When I arrive home, there is an expectation that everyone stops what they are doing and meets me at the door. I have heard it said that the first four minutes in the evening when everyone is home sets the tone for the entire evening. If this is true, I want to use that reunion when I get home to set the tone with positive, healthy physical touch to express love. I do that by hugging them, jumping up and down with them, and kissing them. I do the same with my wife. We carry out this same routine no matter what has gone on during the day and no matter what's going on at home. My family knows when I get home from work and walk in the door, there's a time of reunion that includes healthy physical touch. There's a time of celebration because we know that's what we have to do to build healthy bonds in our home.

In that time, we are saying to each other, "Hey, you're important to me. Of all the things I have going on, no matter what I've dealt with during the day, no matter what I'm feeling stressed about or responsible for, at the end of the day, you are the most important thing to me in the world." When you communicate affection to your spouse or family members, you are telling them they, and their deepest problems and successes, are important to you and you're going to care for and protect them. It tells them you will be there for them when they need you.

Now you know. Physical touch can strengthen connection in your home. Take a step of faith and be more intentional with your touch to communicate love. If you do, your family will grow stronger. You will enjoy life more. And, you will be more able to live as a family on mission with God.

Reflection Questions

- What was your initial reaction to the idea that physical touch is essential to a family living connected on mission for God?

_____

_____

_____

_____

_____

- The science behind the power of touch is pretty impressive. What statement stood out to you the most? Why?

___

- Rate your view of physical touch on a scale of 1 to 5 (1 being "icky" and 5 being "invigorating"). How does your family history affect that rating? How does that rating affect your spouse and children?

___

- Jesus brought the power of touch to new levels in the Gospels. When have you witnessed a time when a simple touch made all the difference for someone?

___

- Evaluate this statement: "as our love for others intensifies, so will our natural expression of love through healthy physical touch." What do you think of this idea, that gospel-induced love overflows in physical touch?

_____
_____
_____
_____

- Of the seven practical steps listed for applying the power of touch, in which one are you doing well? Which one can you begin doing this week?

_____
_____
_____
_____
_____

CHAPTER 6

Living Connected & Money

"You cannot serve God and money." I have heard it said that money is like another person in your home. Over the years as I have prepared people for marriage or sat with people trying to strengthen the connections in their home, I have seen that most people have difficulty in their relationship with this other person. Money can either be a healthy functioning person in your home, or a disruptive pain causing problems. Without a doubt, you must carefully consider how each person in your home relates to money if you want to live connected on mission with God. It is possible that an improper relationship with money will be the greatest obstacle to your family experiencing all that God has for you on mission. If you are overly stressed about money, your energy and resources to fully engage the mission of God will be diminished. My desire is for your families to experience a peaceful home with connected individuals who understand that money is a tool for engaging the mission of God.

Getting Real about Money

Consider these statistics: 100 percent of people need money to live. That's verifiable. If that doesn't capture your attention, how about this one: 0 percent of people can live without food. You may say, "I grow my own food." You still need money to do that. All of us need money to live. So, we cannot ignore the need to properly relate to money.

The major problem in most homes is that most people want to live like money can do more than it was ever meant to do. The majority of people live in debt. Simply put, debt happens when we spend more money than we earn. I won't bore you with statistics. When there is debt, there is stress. When there is stress, families struggle to function in the way that God intends. Some of you are feeling the stress related to your money situation right now in your family relationships.

The Problem of Money Isn't New

When the New Testament was written in the first century, they too had stress related to money. The majority of Jews were poor. Many people were concerned about money, and some people in this culture were manipulating others to gain more money. Some preached purely for money, and others preached that money itself was evil. Many people were confused when it came to money.

In 1 Timothy 6, Paul is writing to Timothy, his protégé. Timothy is a pastor of a new church who is dealing with false teachers. Some false teachers have come into the church, and they are preaching a troubling message about money. Part of that message stated that if you were godly, you would be rich.

I don't regularly call out pastors, but I saw a tweet from Creflo Dollar, who's a prosperity gospel preacher. He tweeted, "Jesus bled and died for us so that we can lay claim to the promise of financial prosperity."[1] That is so far from the truth of the gospel and the truth of the New Testament, it is sick. In fact, I retweeted it. I just said, "Sick." Creflo's people have not called me yet. (Creflo has since deleted this tweet.)

Recently, I was with a couple who expressed a sense of call to start a new church. They already had a name: "Abundant Life Church." As a part of my inquiry, I asked them, "What is your favorite verse in the Bible?"

The man responded, "John 10:10: 'The thief comes only to steal and kill and destroy. I came that they may have life and have it abundantly.'"

"Mine too!" I replied. "But wait. Tell me what this verse means."

They began to reply with an understanding of the verse that went something like this: "The devil wants to take our stuff. But, Jesus gives us stuff."

A sinking feeling hit my stomach. In their understanding of Jesus's words, God is mostly about people being rich. And, they wanted to lead a church teaching people that if your relationship with God is good, you will also have material wealth.

I finally asked, "Can a poor person live an abundant life?"

They were paralyzed by the idea and unable to respond.

Needless to say, I didn't want them starting a new church. This is the kind of thinking that Paul is helping Timothy root out of his church. It is an understanding of God that leaves no room for Jesus, who had no place to lay his head (Luke 9:58). He was not materially rich.

To have a proper relationship with money, we must learn to relate to it in healthy ways. Money cannot, ultimately, meet your deepest needs for connection to God and others. Sure, we all need some. But the reason that many families are financially unstable is that people expect money to do something for them it was never meant to do. We must reject the temptation that money is our greatest need in this life.

Diagnosing Our Contentment

In 1 Timothy, Paul is writing to bring clarity to these early Christians' understanding of money. Instead of connecting godliness with wealth, Paul connects godliness with contentment.

> [6]But godliness with contentment is great gain, [7]for we brought nothing into the world, and we cannot take anything out of the world. [8]But if we have food and clothing, with these we will be content. [9]But those who desire to be rich fall into temptation, into a snare, into many senseless and harmful desires that plunge people into ruin and destruction. [10]For the love of money is a root of all kinds of evils. It is through this craving that some have wandered away from the faith and pierced themselves with many pangs.
>
> 1 Timothy 6:6–10

What do you think about what you already have?
This passage helps us understand how money affects relationships. First, this passage calls us to assess our level of contentment with the things we already have. Here's the question: "Am I okay with what I have?" Verse 6 states that godliness results in contentment with what we have—not a guarantee of having more. *"For we brought nothing into the world,"* Paul says, *"and we cannot take anything out of the world."* What a simple, profound truth.

When you think about the role of money in your home, are you content with what you have? Or when you think about what you have, is there a lingering sense of, "If I just had a little bit more, I would be more happy"? "If I just had a little bit more income, if I had just a few more things, if I just had a little bigger house or a little nicer car or a little more in my 401(k), if I had a little more to invest or put in savings, then I would be okay."

Genuine contentment comes from a God-focused life. If you are looking for a starting place to improve your relationship with money, put your eyes on Jesus. The problem for most of us is that we are overly focused on the stuff we want (and need), making it nearly impossible to experience contentment in whatever financial reality we are living in. There are still things we need—verse 8 states that we need food and clothing. That's true. But beyond that, most of the things we have are not things we need to live, yet these things tend to consume our attention. It is like an addiction. We know expecting money to bring contentment is flawed thinking, but we so easily look to it for contentment.

We can see this quite clearly in our kids. They are never truly satisfied with what money can provide. If you don't believe me, go to Disney World. On our last trip to the happiest place on earth, I can recall more than one moment when a child was complaining about something. I was like, really? "I have saved for twelve months for this trip, and you are complaining? And, I certainly don't like crowds or standing in line! The only reason I am here is to make you happy!" If money could buy contentment, no child would cry at Disney World.

Not only does it cost you valuable energy, time, and relational connection, but an improper relationship with money makes it impossible to think clearly about your future mission with God. All your future decisions become subject to what you earn and what you have. But what if God has something incredible in store for you that requires you to step out in faith financially or make a financial sacrifice? If you are focused solely on money, you will never be content, and you may miss an exciting journey with God.

Some of you have a dysfunctional relationship with money, and it's affecting relationships in your home. It results in fighting over money that is spent or lost. It might pull you away from your family by causing you to work more hours.

There is a familiar verse, Philippians 4:13, that says, "I can do all things through Christ who strengthens me." Just recently I was standing in line behind a man at a popular sporting goods store. I paid extra attention to him, because he had Philippians 4:13 tattooed on his arm. Apparently, he had waited for some time to purchase a

YETI cooler. Personally, I don't get why someone would pay so much money to keep ice cold, but who am I to judge. As he was in line trying to check out, he was noticeably agitated. He underestimated how much money he had and was unable to purchase this expensive cooler. It was so strange, because he wanted this YETI cooler badly and was unable to buy it, causing him to try to negotiate with the salesperson. No luck. After much debating, he stomped out of the store using a few choice words to express his disgust. If only he knew the meaning of the verse he had tattooed on his arm. When Paul writes, "I can do all things through Christ who strengthens me," he's talking about contentment in money. In that passage, he goes on to write about how he has learned to be content with a lot or a little. I wonder how many of us love that verse until we realize its real meaning: "In Christ, I can be content with however much or little money God has provided me."

What do you think about what you'd like to have?
The second thing the passage in 1 Timothy calls us to do is to gauge our desire to be rich. Verse 9 states, "Those who desire to be rich fall into temptation, into a snare, into many senseless and harmful desires that plunge people into ruin and destruction." In Paul's context, he is writing to those Christians who think that because they're godly, they're going to be rich. Their ultimate goal is financial gain. They are focusing on possessions to satisfy a need in their hearts that only God can fill. As we think about money and how it affects our relationships, we have to gauge our desire to be rich.

To be clear, there is good news a little later from Paul to Timothy that it is not wrong to be rich. Amen? There's nothing wrong with working hard and earning a lot of money. In fact, Paul says in 1 Timothy 6:18, "*They* [rich people] *are to do good.*" He assumes there is a group of people who are rich, and he does not tell them they shouldn't be. Instead, he tells those who are rich how they're to live.

You may be rich. In fact, most anyone reading this book is rich compared to people Paul writes to in the first century. About the rich, Paul writes, "They are to do good." They are to be rich in good works—to be generous and ready to share.

So, it's not wrong to be rich, but desiring riches too much will lead you into temptation, into a snare, into many senseless and harmful desires that plunge people into ruin and destruction. Paul is trying to get across, "Be careful. If your desire to gain more possessions is too intense, it will lead you into ruin and destruction. Be warned."

This does not mean we should not work hard. We must work hard. You may say, "Hey, I'm content. I don't want much, so I'm not going to work." That is foolishness. Still, there's a generation of people beginning to talk that way. Proverbs 14:23 NIV says, "*All hard work brings a profit, but mere talk leads only to poverty.*" Rejecting money is just as foolish as being too focused on riches. To work hard is a godly thing.

When you work hard, "unto the Lord" according to Colossians 3, you may find that you have more income. You may be able to purchase more things. There's nothing wrong with that as long as we realize more money gives us greater opportunity to use it to advance God's mission in the world.

If your desire to be rich is healthy, you will become more generous. If your desire to be rich is unhealthy, it will lead you to dishonesty, you'll neglect your family, and you'll justify cheating in your mind because that's what you have to do to get the deal. It will lead you into sin. If you find yourself having to be dishonest to accomplish the work of your hands to gain income, you are on a path to destruction. Gauge your desire to be rich.

We need to be very clear minded on what we love. Will you love God or love money? Pick one. When you've assessed your level of contentment, you may very likely admit that you are not content. You may gauge your desire to be rich and realize that you are going to have to choose between two options: Are you going to love God or love money? You may say, "I don't want to choose just one." You have to.

Look at 1 Tim. 6:10: *"For the love of money is the root of all kinds of evils. It is through this craving that some have wandered away from the faith and pierced themselves with many pangs."* It doesn't say money is evil, but the love of money is the root of all kinds of evil. People who choose to love money believe it will make them happy. The truth is that we follow what we love. What Paul is saying in 1 Timothy is that if you choose money, it is going to lead you away from faith into a place of pain.

Jesus Offers Only Two Choices

Jesus talks a lot about money. Isn't that interesting? He discusses money and possessions more than any other issue during his time on earth. That should prick our hearts to think, "Wow, the way money affects our homes and our relationships must be important."

Jesus says in Matthew 6:24: "*No one can serve two masters, for you will hate one and love the other or you'll be devoted to one and despise the other. You cannot serve both God and money.*" In this passage, Jesus does what is called *animating* money. In other words, money is not just some idea that's out there. Instead, he is positing God as a being and money as a being next to each other. He is saying, "You cannot love both of them. You cannot chase hard after both of these. So pick one."

Here are a few ways to assess whether you love God or love money.

- Do I give generously to what God most cares about?
- Does my pursuit of more money affect my family negatively?
- Do my spending habits require me to work too much?
- Do I have a plan for getting out of debt and living debt free?
- Do I have to be dishonest to make more money or hide spending habits?
- When I am stressed, do I first look to what money can buy or to God for comfort?

How Can I Escape the Idol of Money?

Over the years, I have sat down with many people to help them navigate difficulties in their relationships. Nearly every time a couple is having problems in their marriage or is on the brink of divorce, the problem at the top of the list is money. Every time, I ask them this: "Well, do you love God?" They nearly always say yes. Then I say, "Are you being a generous person?" Rarely are people living as generously as they hope to be.

Then I ask, "Do you have a budget?" This is so simple. Here's my call to action. The most practical, powerful thing you can do as it relates to finances in your home is to set a budget. Almost every time, they say something like this: "Yes, we have a budget. She pays the bills." Or, "Yes, we have a budget. He pays the bills." Or maybe they say, "We know how much is in our checking account because we looked at it this morning." That is not a budget.

If you say, "I choose to love God," the first thing you do with the resources that God has provided for you is think about how you are going to use them. How are you going to live? If you're spending more money than you make, there may be a problem, and you may need to make an adjustment in your lifestyle.

I would bet my own money—I'm actually not going to because it's not part of my budget—but I would bet that a very small percentage of people reading this have an actual budget. That means at the beginning of the month, you're telling all of your money where to go. This is one of the most important things I teach about as a pastor as I try to point people to love God fully and have healthy relationships in their homes.

To live within your budget, you may need to make more money. Making more money could even provide more dollars so that you can live into your passion for helping others. For some of you, that may mean you need to work more. You may need to find a different job. There is nothing wrong with that. Wanting to make more money does not necessarily mean you love money. In fact, you may look at where God is leading you with your family and realize, "We need more money to do this, so I'm willing to be open to what God is calling me to do in the next season of my life so that I can make more money." There's nothing wrong with that, as long as your desire to be rich is not greater than your desire to be godly.

To live within your budget, you may need to make more money, but most need to learn how to spend less. To spend less money, you have to realize that there is a place in your heart that will never be filled by the things of this world. It can only be met by the Lord Jesus Christ.

The Gospel Transforms Our View of Money
The Bible teaches really good news. The good news is that in the beginning, after all things were perfect and in order, man sinned. Man rebelled against God and sin entered the world. Sin affects all of us, and we all sense that something in us is empty. We live our lives trying to meet that need. The good news of the gospel is that the only way the deepest need of your heart will be met is through a real relationship with God. Because our sin separates us from God, the only way we become children of God and enter into a real relationship with him is through Jesus Christ. When God sent Jesus to die on a cross, he paid for our sin. This is the gospel. As Christians, we believe that a real relationship with God through Jesus Christ is the only thing that will meet our deepest need. Money will not meet your deepest needs.

If you do not believe that, then you need a lot of money. You need to purchase a lot of things to keep chasing that feeling of happiness. But it won't last, so you're going to need more money, and that is going to negatively affect your relationships.

The Gospel Shows Us Our Greatest Need
Ask yourself, "Do I believe that God can meet my deepest needs?" If so, can you think more clearly about how much money you spend? Evaluate whether you need to be spending so much money on food or a certain home or a type of clothes. Do you have the money for these things? Recognize that maybe you just need to spend less because at the end of the day, those things aren't going to make you happy or meet your deepest need.

Maybe you need to work more, maybe you need to spend less, or maybe you can even sell some stuff—that is a very practical thing. And to live within your budget, you may need help from someone who can advise you. Find somebody who cares enough about your spiritual wellbeing and knows enough about finances to help you make a budget. I often point people in my church to Dave Ramsey's Financial Peace University, a program designed to help you live within your budget.

The Gospel Drives Us to Passionate Generosity
I'll leave it to the professionals to teach you how to create your budget.[2] But I believe that if we love God, the first item on our budgets should be this—generosity. Often, it's the last item, but as you grow in godliness and contentment, generosity will move from being the last item to the first item. When people love God, they give generously to the work of God in the world.

Where do you see God working? Give to that generously. If you see God working in some organization outside the life of the church, give to it. If you see God working in the life of your church, give to it. That is an area of obedience. It's not an option if you are in Christ. We give generously because we care about what God cares about in the world.

Budget line item number one—not number ten or fifteen or twenty or thirty—is this: give generously. Ask yourself, where am I going to give generously toward God's work in this world? If you choose to live generously, it will strengthen connections in your home. Why? Because, you are investing in something much larger than yourselves. And, it will strengthen your connections with one another as God excites your hearts toward his mission in the world.

My Guarantee for Those Who Love God

Here's what success looks like. If you do these things, if you assess your level of contentment, if you're honest with yourself, if you gauge your desire for riches, and then you choose to love God, here is a guarantee.

Your Stress Will Decrease

I guarantee there will be fewer stresses in your home related to money. If you choose God and there are not fewer stresses in your home, let me know.

Your Kids Will Grow

Another success is that you will be able to teach your kids about money, not just with your words but also with your lifestyle. One of the most important lessons we can teach our kids is when we want to buy something, saying, "You know what? We did not plan for that in the budget. God's not provided that money, so we're not going to do it. We trust that God has provided everything we need for life and godliness."

One reason some people have a dysfunctional relationship with money as adults is that they grew up in homes with parents who had an unhealthy relationship with money. You will spend money like your parents spent money. I know I do. I grew up in a home with very conservative spending habits. At times, I hated it. For instance, I grew up wearing off-brand shoes and clothes. I can remember as a kid being ridiculed by other kids for the types of shoes I wore. I wore Pro Wings: a cheap, uncool, plain-looking shoe. In fact, I can remember my first pair of Nikes like it was yesterday. I got them in the ninth grade. I had suffered through eight years of Pro Wings when finally the heavens opened and I got some Nike Air Delta Force ST Low shoes. They were high performance low top shoes for "serious players." I was a size eight. Every day after school, I would come home and sponge clean those things to keep them in tip-top shape. I think I wore those things through my foot growing to a size 10. Even now, I appreciate a good pair of shoes but am unwilling to spend too much on a pair. That is the house I grew up in. It set in me an appreciation for every dollar spent.

One reason my parents were so conservative in their spending is that their greatest joy was to spend money on things that pleased God. Every Sunday, they put a check in the offering plate at church. I didn't understand it at the time, but looking back I realize my parents spent conservatively on temporary things but were incredibly generous on eternal things.

Your Reward Will Be Eternal

If you choose to love God and become a generous person, you will get to see God use your money for an eternal reward. So when you breathe your last breath, you will know that the investment you've made in what God is doing in the world throughout the course of your life will last beyond your life.

Maybe you see yourself someday living in another part of the world because you believe God wants you to go there and share the love of Christ with people who don't have access to the gospel. Can you imagine being in a place where you can take that step of faith because your decisions aren't dependent on money?

Maybe you want to make a career change. You do not feel passionate about what you're doing at work, and you're ready to make a move. Can you imagine being in a place where your step of faith into a new career would contribute to society and honor God? Can you imagine taking that step of faith without it being dependent upon money? I hope that you will see that as success.

Your Faith Will Grow

One last sign of success when you love God and allow it to affect your finances is that you will be able to take steps of faith that are not dependent on money. What a freeing place to be.

In my life, God has led me to take some leaps of faith. One of those was when God put in our hearts to start a new church in urban Houston. When we decided to step out in faith, we had no money. None. But, I knew that God would provide. And he has provided. What's more, everything we have gone without are things we could never take into eternity. It is an incredibly freeing place to be.

As your faith grows, you will more boldly live on mission as a family. As you and your house take steps of faith financially to serve the Lord, you will experience great joy in life. Listen carefully. Life on mission isn't possible without a bold faith free from the idol of money. Reread that sentence. It's true.

My Guarantee for Those Who Love Money

If you don't do these things, here's the failure: you will drift. You will drift in your relationships with God and your family. Your home relationships will be strained, will be stressed, and will be broken. So, what will you do? How will you think about money? Loving God allows money to strengthen family relationships, not weaken them.

How the Gospel Transformed My View of Money

Honestly, I waffle back and forth between focusing on money and focusing on God. My sense of contentment is always affected by where my focus is. By God's grace, on more than one occasion when my eyes were focused on God, God led my family to take a financial step of faith in the next step of his mission. This was certainly true when we moved from suburban Houston to inner city Houston. At the time, I didn't know God would lead me to start a new church, but I knew God was sending us into a very unreached area of Houston to live out our Christian faith. It didn't make financial sense. I like to say, "It was faith risky, not stupid risky." To pay the difference in the cost of living between the burbs and the inner city, I started a delivery business that required I get up earlier and make deliveries before work five days a week. It was tough, but I knew God would provide. After a year of living in the city, God put on our hearts to start a new church. At this point, I had to make a choice. Will I focus on God? Or, will I focus on the financial risk, the impending bills, and the uncertainty of my financial future? And, more than one person said, "You are an idiot." But we became gripped with a sense of mission. By God's grace, we stepped into the unknown. In looking back over this season that required more faith than I ever thought possible, I would do it all again. Sure, God has used it to impact other families. But the greatest impact has been on our own family. We now have a real-life story proving all that the Bible reveals about money. God will provide. Wealth is not more important than godliness, and lasting joy is given by God—not money.

Reflection Questions

- Imagine "money" as a person in your family. How does each member of the family relate with him? How often does he interrupt your conversations? How has he helped or hindered your family's life on mission for God?

- How do you tend to think of your relationship with money as unique? In what ways do your challenges with money compare or contrast with challenges that existed for people in the Bible?

- Define contentment in your own words. How does contentment affect how you view what you already have? How does contentment shape how you view what you'd like to have in the future?

- Think of a time in your life when your idolatry of money was most evident. What were some symptoms of this idolatry? In what ways did you feel entrapped?

- Spend ten minutes in prayer, thanking God for the freeing power of the gospel. In preparation for your prayer time, ask yourself how the gospel has freed you from the idol of money. How does the gospel change your understanding of your greatest need? Read Romans 8:31–39 and 2 Corinthians 9:6–15. How does the gospel change your view of giving as it did the view of New Testament Christians?

- Do you have a family budget? If not, take some time to build one this week. If you do, take a few minutes and examine how it is structured. What does your budget communicate about your priorities?

_____
_____
_____
_____
_____

- What step of faith would you like to take individually or as a family that is prevented by your idolatry of money?

_____
_____
_____
_____
_____
_____
_____

CHAPTER 7

Living Connected & Rest

A story is told of an exploring party who had employed a group of native Inca carriers to go with them into the mountains. Being in a hurry to reach their objective, the party was pushed relentlessly for several days. Finally, the natives just sat down and would go no farther. Asked what was the matter, the superstitious natives replied, "We had been moving too fast and had to wait for our souls to catch up."[1]

If I asked you to list three words to describe your life, what would they be? Most people I ask have "busy" on the list. We live in a culture that forfeits rest for work and play—the average person is tired. But we don't have to live in this way. Actually, if we neglect rest, we will injure our bodies and our souls. And it will hurt not only us, but it will hurt our families.

The reason I wrote this book is to help families live connected on mission with God. I believe most Christians really do want to experience God using them to impact their world, but the chronic disconnect in the home keeps them from seeing their desire become a reality. If I had to pick the most troublesome reality keeping our families from getting on mission, it would be that we neglect rest. In the next few pages, I want to help you see how God has established rest as an essential part to healthy living. I will then offer a few simple ways you can adjust your weekly rhythms to make room for rest.

In the Beginning . . . God Rested
God rested. We read this mind-boggling truth in the creation account recorded in Genesis. Honestly, this statement strikes me as hard to believe. It's hard to believe because God had a lot of work to do. In six days ("periods of time"...whatever, let's not lose the point of the passage by debating this one), God brought form and function to all that had no form and no function. He spoke into existence the earth we live on and get food from, the animals we barbecue and enjoy as pets, the waters we swim in and the stars we gaze at, and so many other wonderful things. Everything God created was good. Then, he did something "very good" by creating the first humans. The distinct difference between humans and everything else is that we are created "in the image of God." After all this work, God rested (Genesis 2:2). As some theologians have helpfully put it, "The language is anthropomorphic, for God is not a weary workman in need of rest. Nevertheless, the pattern is here set for man to follow."[2] In the beginning, before sin disrupted life, rest was natural.

Fast forward to the Ten Commandments that God gives to Israel. This list includes things like, "don't murder," "don't lie," and "don't have sex with someone who is not your spouse." It's a very clear list to help God's people understand how they are to love God and love others. Of all the serious commands, the one requiring the most words to clearly communicate how we should live is about rest.

> [8]*Remember the Sabbath day, to keep it holy.* [9]*Six days you shall labor, and do all your work,* [10]*but the seventh day is a Sabbath to the* LORD *your God. On it you shall not do any work, you, or your son, or your daughter, your male servant, or your female servant, or your livestock, or the sojourner who is within your gates.* [11] *For in six days the* LORD *made heaven and earth, the sea, and all that is in them, and rested on the seventh day. Therefore the* LORD *blessed the Sabbath day and made it holy.*
> —Exodus 20:8–11

A day of rest was a natural part of God's original plan. Sin disrupted this plan. In this passage, God has to command his people to rest. Read this carefully: Our tendency to neglect rest is a result of the fall and sin entering into humanity. God says, "For six days, work hard. For one day, rest from work." Consider this: in the same list of commands that says we should not inflict pain on another person by lying, stealing, or murdering, is the command to rest weekly. It seems to me that neglecting rest is choosing to inflict pain on yourself. Not only does neglecting rest hurt ourselves, but it hurts others.

The commands of God are for our wellbeing. As a dad, I have the awesome responsibility of setting rules in our home. When my kids were very young, I commanded them not to touch the hot stovetop. They might not have understood the seriousness of obeying this command, but I knew how badly the stove could hurt them. I set this as a rule in our home for their wellbeing. If, however, they chose to disobey this command, they would have suffered the consequences. I can see what they cannot easily see as a child. It's important for them to learn to obey me.

Can you imagine that God's command to rest is for your wellbeing? You might not fully understand how you can get along in life with a weekly rhythm of rest, but I hope you will trust God. If you neglect rest, you will injure yourself. You will injure others in your family because your rhythms affect everyone else in your home.

How You Rest Declares What You Believe about the Gospel

In our weekly choice to obey this command to rest, we are doing more than just taking time off of work. We are acknowledging that there will be a day when all striving on earth will be complete. We will enter an eternal rest having received the full inheritance of our salvation in Christ. This rest is made possible by Jesus Christ (Hebrews 4:9–11). We are also acknowledging that our hope in life is not in ourselves, but we trust in God to take care of us even on days when we aren't working. He is working while we rest. Last, we are setting aside a day to recover physically and focus spiritually. Typically, we attend church on this day of rest. To be clear, rest is about so much more than just clocking out from work. There is some significant work that is done in our souls when we obey God's command to rest.

I wonder how many of you are weary. If you are like most people I know, you need rest. I know I do. Making time to rest will not come without a fight for it. Of course, you can reject God's command to rest, but you will suffer for it.

Just a few years ago, I was heavily involved in triathlon racing. I got into it with the encouragement from some friends, and I really enjoyed that season of competing. When I started, I did shorter races (consisting of a 400-yard swim, 20-mile bike ride, and 3-mile run). As my love for the sport grew, I began to set my eyes on training for an Ironman distance triathlon race (a 2.4-mile swim, 112-mile bike ride, and 26.3-mile run). To train, I knew that I'd need to slowly add miles to each discipline to prepare for one day of putting it all together. I learned things about nutrition, equipment, and strategy. But, the most important thing I learned was the value of rest, including rest in my workout plan. This rest felt counterintuitive because I had to get ready for what would be a very long race. When I started, I knew I needed to lose weight, run faster, swim faster, and pedal harder if I was going to finish in the allotted seventeen hours to complete all these distances.

But at some point in the year leading up to my training, I began to experience a slight pain in my foot. Keep in mind, I had already signed up for the race, booked the trip, and gotten all my equipment. As I continued to train, the pain got continually worse. I was several thousand dollars and many hours of training into preparing for this race. I decided to go the orthopedic doctor to find out why I could not recover from my nagging injury. After a series of questions about nutrition and workout routine, the doctor asked, "How often do you rest?"

Um, rarely. I had work to do. I neglected rest. I was overworking in an effort to get to the finish line.

But after the doctor's visit, I began taking more time off from my training during the next couple of months. My injury healed, and on race day I was in the best shape of my life. By God's grace and with the encouragement of many onlookers, I finished the Ironman in thirteen hours and forty minutes. I will never forget the words announced for all to hear, "Russell Cravens, YOU are an Ironman!" Of all the things I learned during that period of triathlon training, there is none more lasting than what I learned about rest. If I had not learned to rest, I would not have finished. Period.

I think most Christians who neglect rest are sincerely wanting to reach the finish line in their life with Christ. None of us want to get injured and step out of the race altogether. But the reality is that some of you will. You will quit the race God has marked for you because you neglect rest. I get it. You are busy. You have work to do. Your employer needs you. Your kids need you. Your friends need you. Your hobbies need you. But, the busyness of those things is literally killing you. Stop it. God knows what you need to live well, and he has made it quite clear that rest is essential to finish your race.

I am guessing you can easily identify the areas of your schedule that are too busy with work and play and prevent you from resting. But, there may be some fatigue in your heart. Merely changing your weekly routine will not satisfy the restlessness in that place. In his book

Confessions, St. Augustine points to the real solution to the problem of human restlessness, when he says, "Thou hast made us for Thyself and our hearts are restless until they find rest in Thee."[3] You see, there is a rest needed in our hearts that can only be satisfied by Jesus. Life will exhaust you without Jesus in your life.

Jesus invites the weary into a kind of rest that is uniquely his, saying, "Come to me, all who labor and are heavy laden, and I will give you rest. Take my yoke upon you, and learn from me, for I am gentle and lowly in heart, and you will find rest for your souls. For my yoke is easy, and my burden is light" (Matthew 11:28–30). I am wondering as I write about how weary you are in your soul. Maybe others don't notice. In fact, if you are showing up to your job and home to check off the boxes for each role, most people won't notice when you become soul-weary. But Jesus invites us all to come to him for rest in our souls. This is not the promise an ordinary teacher would make.[4]

We are not without responsibility in accepting this invitation. Our part is to take his yoke on. The imagery here uses two oxen. A yoke is the wooden collar that connects the two together. So, taking on this yoke means that we submit ourselves to the way of Jesus Christ. The alternatives are to take on the yoke of the world or (in this context) of religious legalism. The only one of these that gives rest to the soul is to take on the way of Jesus Christ. There we will find rest for our souls.

How to Rest When Life Is Chaotic

You might say, "Okay, I get it. I need to rest. How?" Good question. I am convinced that looking to the way of the Hebrew people helps us think clearly about how rest should be a regular part of our lives. I have already shown you how the command to uphold a Sabbath requires we stop work weekly to rest. This day of rest was given by God to serve us (Mark 2:27). It serves us by enabling us to more effectively do our work the other six days of the week. The spirit of the command is so that we experience peace in life with God. In Jewish tradition, there is a name for this: "Shabbat shalom"—literally, "may your day of no work be peaceful." One person would say this as a greeting to another, and that person would respond in kind: "May your day of no work be peaceful as well."[5] This will sound strange to most of us because we work without rest.

I love to work. I really do. I have been fortunate to work in a job I really love. As a pastor, there is always something to do. Early in ministry, I prided myself on showing up early and staying late to prepare sermons, organize events, manage the budget, and counsel people. As I've already mentioned several times in this book, my most recent work has been to start a new church in the urban core of Houston, Texas. When we began, I knew it would be a lot of work. I was ready, and I have enjoyed much of this last season of work. But, it has been hard. Just a couple years into this church plant, something really scary began happening. I couldn't stay asleep. I could easily fall asleep after exhausting myself during the day, but I would wake in the middle of the night with my mind racing. It was like I would start the day at race level RPMs and stay at that intensity all day. I fueled with a lot of caffeine.

But, I began feeling exhausted. I was on edge, and it was affecting my relationships at home. I had little energy to be present with my wife and kids. Sure, I was going through the motions as a husband and dad. But I was living in surface level connection with everyone around me, including God. I became miserable. And the scary part was that no one knew. Occasionally, my more discerning friends would say, "Russ, you look tired." I'd usually reply with a super-spiritual reply like, "I'll rest when I die." Ironically, my pace was pushing up that timeline considerably. I was literally working myself into an early grave. I worked at work. I thought about work at home. On my days not in the office, I was checking my phone, taking calls, trying to connect with people outside the church, and dreaming of how to be better at work.

To be fair, my intensity at work was not because anyone was asking more of me. I was completely in charge of my own schedule, and I still neglected rest. Sure, I took a day off. But, on my days off, I didn't cease from my non-paying work (house chores, kid's activities, etc.) to rest. And as I mentioned, no one called me out on it. I have some great people around me who love me very much, but here is what I know: no one will choose rest for you. In fact, you will not be applauded by most for choosing to rest weekly. There is rarely accountability in our discipleship models for obeying God's command to observe the Sabbath. This is a problem. Lack of rest is not only affecting us, but it is negatively impacting our families. I became a shell of a person. I knew if I didn't take some extended time off from work, I was in trouble. So, I took an extended period away from work to recover. In reflection, I was more tired than I realized. And, it was slowly killing me, my marriage, and the connection with my kids.

My situation reminds me of a Greek legend set in ancient Athens. As the legend goes, a man noticed the great storyteller Aesop playing childish games with some little boys. He laughed and jeered at Aesop, asking him why he wasted his time in such frivolous activity.

Aesop responded by picking up a bow, loosening its string, and placing it on the ground. Then he said to the critical Athenian, "Now, answer the riddle, if you can. Tell us what the unstrung bow implies."

The man looked at it for several moments but had no idea what point Aesop was trying to make. Aesop explained, "If you keep a bow always bent, it will break eventually; but if you let it go slack, it will be more fit for use when you want it."

Resting a bow string is easy; resting in the midst of a chaotic life is tough.

Fight for Time Off

Since getting back to a more normal work routine, I have had to fight for days (and periods) off from work. I still can let weeks pass without taking time to let my soul recover in the presence of the Lord. There is always work to be done, and if I worked more, my "business" would grow faster. Or, at least that is the voice still in my head. Maybe working seven days a week on the job God has given us will, in reality, negatively impact the result if we neglect rest. I think this is why God commands rest. He knows the way he made us. We are made in his image, and if he rested we should also.

Not too long ago, I gave a sermon to my church on the need for weekly rhythms of rest. As I looked out over the audience, I saw working moms, graduate students, business owners, and oil executives. The thought occurred to me, "No one believes what I am saying is possible." This feeling was affirmed as I chatted with people after church who gave me that "cute sermon, not reality" look we sometimes get as preachers. I was a bit stunned by the reality in our culture that we believe rest is impossible. We are living at a frenetic pace, and it has become completely normalized. How can we expect to build meaningful connections with others (most importantly in our homes) when we are exhausting ourselves with work and non-restful play? Deep, meaningful connections require slowing down to be present with others. They require energy. They require time. And we are allowing work to deplete both time and energy. Stop it.

I have said repeatedly that I am writing with the strong assumption that most Christians want to be about the mission of God in the world. You have heard your pastor say, "God wants to use you for his glory." You believe it. But, you walk out of church and nothing changes. Why? It is because some things need to be worked on in your home? Without working on these things like affection, words, anger, etc., you will never fully engage with others in your home to get on mission with God. Think about this: you might be neglecting the other areas in your lives because you are too tired or too busy to give them the needed time. We need rest. Neglecting rest will lead to injury in every area of your life.

Discover What Depletes You

You might have picked up on what I include as work. Certainly, I am talking about working at your job. But, busying ourselves by entertaining ourselves and others can be included in what I have in mind as work. We need to think about how to find rest from anything that depletes our energies. You know what that is for you. For me, there are things that I enjoy doing that include other people. But, if it's something that requires an exertion of energy, I will still need to plan for times of rest. On the other hand, things like exercising, hunting, or reading are ways that I rest. For some, these things will feel like work. It's okay. The point is, you must spend some time thinking about what depletes your energy and what you do that feels restful. Rest from things that deplete your energy by spending entire days on those things.

Discover What Refreshes You

Another thing I try to do on my day off is exercise. This doesn't feel like work to me. I enjoy it. This will sound strange to those of you who hate exercising, but I feel really connected to God when I am caring for my own body. It was given to me by God, so I imagine he is honored when I care for it. Last, I try to nap on my day of rest. This is impossible during a busy work week. It just makes sense that we will nap on the day we are given by God to cease from work. Sleeping is the exact opposite of working. This is what I do, but for my wife, reading a good book or sharing a good meal is how she feels most connected to herself and God. Those aren't mine, but I work to create space so she can do those things and rest.

Budget Your Rest

I have found the best way to prioritize rest is to think of it like a financial budget. The difference in the two is that you know exactly how much time you will have every week for the rest of your life. Time is fixed, so you can budget without any variable of how much of it you will have. Only you know what life requires you to give time to, but some things ought to be on every one of our schedules.

Rest weekly. I've already given you my argument for why you need to put rest on your calendar. I believe if you don't put it on your calendar, you will neglect it. Think in terms of an entire 24-hour period where you stop all work activity. Give it to the Lord. In doing so, you unchain yourself from enslavement to work. Truly, rest is a gift from God (Exodus 16:29).

If you are going to budget rest well, you are going to have to learn how to say no to some good options for spending your time. It is okay to say no to some invitations. It is okay to say no to your children's request to be involved in more things. Say it out loud: "It's okay to say no." When you say no to some things, you will be able to say yes to the most important things.

Worship in Your Rest

Remember, this day is set aside as a time for us to recover from work and prepare for work. The most effective way to do these things is by giving the day to the Lord. What does that kind of day look like for you?

Included on this day should be time to gather with other believers for worship. Consider Hebrews 10:24–25, "Let us consider how to stir up one another to love and good works, not neglecting to meet together, as is the habit of some, but encouraging one another, and all the more as you see the Day drawing near." A priority for believers in the early church was gathering weekly for worship. Sadly, when many families need rest, they rest from attending church. Of course, there are times when staying home from worship to rest is appropriate, but the Sabbath is a day to be set aside for the Lord. Gathering with other believers for worship is essential. I hope you have or can find a church where you are invited to experience restoration from six days of work. Another way of looking at it is that gathering with the church to prepare you for the upcoming six days of work is the only way you will be able to do the work God has prepared for you. If you neglect gathering with the church regularly, you will communicate to your family that rest requires distancing yourself from God and the gift of his Body, the Church. When, in fact, the kind of rest we most need can only come from God.

    At some point early on in our church plant, I noticed one previously committed family had only been gathering with us one Sunday a month. This went on for several months, and I decided it was time to talk to the dad. I will never forget our conversation. In it he said, "I'd rather be in bed thinking about church than in church thinking about bed." Frankly, I didn't know how to respond. As it turned out, he was grateful I took the time to reach out to him. We talked for some time about all the time we spend working in addition to our jobs just to keep up with life. The root of the problem we discovered was that they had allowed their schedules to become so busy that every person in the family (including the kids) were running on fumes. I said, "Have you considered that missing church is making you more tired?" You see, the kind of rest we most need is in our souls. Certainly, you can and should find this rest on your own with personal time with God during the week. But there is something supernatural and unique about the way God works in our souls as we gather with the church. When budgeting your time, you must prioritize time to gather with the church. In doing so, you will find much needed rest.

There are other ways you'll find that enable you to connect with the Lord. For some, it's extended Bible reading and study. That can be a good thing if it feels restful to you. For some, reading the Bible feels like work. If it does, I'd suggest you not do it on your day of rest.[6] You see, the problem for some Christians is that you read the Bible because you know you should, but it feels like work. When I say, "Give the day to the Lord," you immediately fill in your task list of spiritual things to do, like Bible reading. But if it feels like work, don't do it. Instead, do some thinking about what you can do that will help you feel connected to God. For me, it is slowing my pace and trying to notice more times in my day that God is present in my life. In my work week, I am usually moving so fast that I don't stop to notice how God is working in my kids. But, on my day of rest, I give myself time to think about ways I am seeing God reveal himself to my children.

Listen to Your Laugh
Another thing I do is allow myself more freedom in laughter. I imagine that when Israel ceased from work

weekly and for festivals (see below), there was a lot of laughter.

As I shared earlier, I recently had to take some extended time away from work. Leading up to this time, I had a lot of prep work to do. On a day when I was questioning whether or not I really needed this time of rest, Jeanie said something that sealed my thinking on the matter. She said, "You don't laugh anymore." For me, this was scary because I have always loved to laugh and make others laugh. It has become a litmus test for me on how rested I am. So, on my days off, I try to give myself space to laugh. This means that we watch shows that make us laugh. I spend extra time playing games with the kids that bring laughter into our home. I give myself to talking with Jeanie about oddities that are funny. I slow down to enjoy the lighter things of life that bring a smile to my face. It's what works for me.

Develop Seasons of Rest

We often need to rest for longer periods of time. In addition to a day each week set aside for rest and worship to the Lord, Israel was prohibited from customary work somewhere around seventy days a year. Each of these was connected to a religious festival. I have in mind here Rosh Hashanah, Yom Kippur, Festival of Purim, Passover, and others.[7] God established these longer periods of rest to focus Israel on specific ways they were to relate to God. In the same way, we ought to plan longer periods of rest throughout the year. I have found it meaningful to calendar at least two days each quarter as time away from ordinary work to rest and reflect on God. You will have to make it work for you, but I enjoy going anywhere where I can lie on a hammock in the woods. Being anywhere outdoors outside of the city feels restful to me. Whenever possible, I will include my family for a couple days away from our normal routine. I am sure you can also think of some way to spend a couple of days each quarter resting from work, but it won't happen unless you plan it in advance.

For longer periods away, I have to get out of Houston. I can't be in Houston and not think about my work. We save up vacation days throughout the year and get away for longer periods. If you are traveling with kids, you might not find these trips all that restful. It's okay to admit it. Be honest with yourself for the wellbeing of your own soul. But, you should try to find at least one longer period during the year when you cease from ordinary work to allow your soul to catch up to your body.

Work out of Your Rest

Discover how to work out of your rest. That's different than the way we typically think about it. We think of rest as being what happens after we work. But, if you will shift this mindset, I believe you will more fully enjoy the work God has given you to do. And in doing so you will be more able to live connected with others on mission.

It reminds me of the story of the woodsmen that goes something like this.

One man challenged another to an all-day wood chopping contest. The challenger worked very hard, stopping only for a brief lunch break. The other man had a leisurely lunch and took several breaks during the day. At the end of the day, the challenger was surprised and annoyed to find that the other fellow had chopped substantially more wood than he had. "I don't get it," he said. "Every time I checked, you were taking a rest, yet you chopped more wood than I did." "But you didn't notice," said the winning woodsman. "My ax was being sharpened when I sat down to rest."

When you faithfully obey God's command to rest, he sharpens you. You are more able to live out of your rest so that you can fully participate in the mission of God in the world. No one will choose this rest for you, but your family is counting on you to lead the way. Your one day of rest prepares you for another six days of mission. So, invite your family into the delightful rhythm of the rest of your Heavenly Father.

Reflection Questions

- How do you schedule time off? What prevents you from taking time away from your work? What (perhaps seemingly counterintuitive) steps might you need to take in order to get more true time away from work than you are presently?

_____

_____

_____

_____

_____

LIVING CONNECTED & REST

- List five activities that deplete you and five activities that refresh you. Have your spouse and children do the same and compare notes. How can your family create space for everyone to avoid depleting activity and enjoy refreshing activity one day a week? If you're struggling to think of refreshing activities, it may mean that you are in the habit of neglecting rest.

_____

_____

_____

_____

_____

_____

_____

- What are some activities that inhibit your rest budget? What responsibilities do you need to decline in order to prioritize rest?

_____

_____

_____

_____

_____

_____

- Think about your last vacations. How did you use these as times to worship? Did your rest take you away from worship in a church setting? In what ways can you ensure that your times of rest are also times of worship?

  _____
  _____
  _____

- Ask your spouse or a close friend to rank how happy you seem on a scale of 1–10 (1 being miserable and 10 being your usual self). Use this as one gauge of how rested you are.

  _____
  _____
  _____

- It's time to mark the calendar. When can you schedule longer periods of vacation or a slower pace at work? Find a spot and put it on the family calendar.

  _____
  _____
  _____

Summary and Invitation to Mission

I believe that most Christians want God to use them for good in the world. When you hear someone say, "God has a special purpose for your life," I imagine your heart leaps with joy. I also believe that many people fritter away their lives, paralyzed by feeling disconnected from their own story and others in their home. It doesn't have to be this way. My prayer is that we would experience God in such a way through his word that we would be transformed from being separated, self-focused individuals into healthy families connected on mission. What we've seen as we examine our own hearts is that we all have problems that disrupt this ideal—the ideal that we will have healthy families connected deeply on mission.

Living Connected as a Result of Transformation

We are all in a process. The anger, the words, conflict, affection, money, and need for rest are all real parts of family life. Maybe you're sitting there reflecting on these chapters and thinking, "You got me. I have an issue with anger," or, "You got me. My words are not always edifying. Sometimes they take life instead of giving life." Maybe you're thinking, "I'm not too good at conflict," or, "I'm not really the affectionate type," or, "Money seems to be a distraction for me." And, I feel almost certain that most of you read the chapter on rest and said, "Guilty!" If any of these areas sound like you, take comfort in the fact that we all face these issues. I certainly do.

Please read this carefully: every one of us needs transformation in areas we cannot change by ourselves. In fact, as I prepared these chapters, I realized that there are places in my life—how I use my words, how I engage or avoid conflict, how I express physical affection to my wife and even my kids—that I have been unable to change. I have tried for many years. The older I get, the more I am convinced that my only real hope for lasting transformation is to invite God to enter my messy heart and get to work. I hope you will do the same.

Living Connected with a New Family
What can you do to experience that much-needed transformation? Jesus has an amazing plan to invite you into God's family. There are two ways to get into a family. You're either born into it, or you're adopted into it. Jesus allows both of these things to happen for us by reconciling us with the Heavenly Father. The sin that separates you from God is erased when, by faith, you choose to acknowledge your sin before God and ask God to forgive your sin. The needed forgiveness is made possible by

Jesus Christ, who paid the penalty for your sin. When he was raised from the dead, you were given the hope of a new life in God's family.

One way the Bible describes this conversion is by being born again. John 1:12–13 says, "To all who did receive him, who believed in his name,"—not just believed that a guy named Jesus existed, but believed in who he is and what he did—"he gave the right to become children of God, who were born, not of blood nor of the will of the flesh nor of the will of man, but of God." Everyone is invited to be a part of God's family by way of being born again into this new family. Through faith your sin goes to him and his righteousness is credited to you. You're born into a new life with a new family, the family of God. No longer are you an enemy of God. In Christ, you're a child of God. You're adopted into God's family.

Maybe as you have been reading this book, sin has been exposed. I know it has been in my own life. We've all lashed out in anger. We've used our words wrongly. We've neglected healthy physical touch, we've loved money more than God, and we've neglected rest. Those things don't just separate our earthly relationships; they separate us from God. God made a way to bridge that separation through Jesus Christ. That's the good news of the Bible. Our sin can be forgiven. We can be born again into the family of God through Christ.

As a part of this family, you get a new opportunity to build the kind of family that has purpose. You may be doing all you can just to create a family where you will still enjoy your spouse and your kids in twenty, thirty, or forty years, but something still seems to be missing, and you're wondering what to do. You and I both need to place our eyes on Jesus.

We need to think more often about what it means to be connected to the Father, to be part of the family of God, and to allow the gospel to seep down into our hearts. Then we will think more carefully about our words. We will begin to realize that money is not going to meet our deepest need for happiness. We will choose rest.

We will see God begin to transform us into the kind of people who show up in our homes in a way that gives life. It will allow us to experience a healthy connection with our spouses. If you're not married, it will prepare you to be the kind of person who can stand at the altar and commit your life to someone, saying in good faith before God, "Hey, I'm not perfect, but I'm in process because I am a part of the family of God."

Jesus made it possible, in spite of the difficulties of his own earthly family, for people to be invited into the family of God. This is our celebration. This is a wonderful gift that God gives us through Christ.

Here is your final call to action. Jesus has invited you into the family—into his family. Have you accepted? Have you crossed over the line of faith? I'm not asking you if you've gone to church. I do a lot of premarital counseling with couples who are not part of a church community. I always ask them to tell me about their faith background, and every single time they begin to tell me about what they did as a child related to church. "Well, my parents didn't go to church," or, "My parents were this denomination," and so on. I have to get past that and say, "No, I'm not talking about that. What I'm talking about is how you relate to God the Father. Have you turned from your sin and turned toward Jesus as the way to become a part of the family of God?"

Sitting in a church as a child does no more to make you into a follower of Christ than sitting in your garage would make you into a car. You need God to rescue you from your sin. You need to cross the line into the family of God by faith. Have you been made at peace with God? If you have not done that, then you have not taken the first step necessary for you to show up in relationships in a healthy way. Have you crossed over the line of faith?

Living Connected with Others

You cannot do it alone. Your family cannot do it alone. One powerful reality of the local church is that it provides a new kind of larger family for us to connect with on mission. A pastor friend of mine inspires his church with two simple words: "Better together." When your family lives connected on mission with others, you will more clearly see areas of your life that need to be better. Also, you will multiply your impact in the neighborhoods God is sending you.

Living Connected on Mission

God is constantly inviting people into his family on mission. The ultimate goal is not just that you would experience deeper relationships in your home. I want that for you. But ultimately, we want deeper family relationships so that we can be on a mission in a way that impacts the neighborhoods and cities and the world we live in.

A favorite story of mine is about a daredevil named Clifford Calverly. He astounded his audience by pushing a wheelbarrow over a tightrope stretched across Niagara Falls. After performing this feat, he turned to the crowds, who were awestruck by this incredible feat of courage. He asked, "Now that you've seen what I can do, do you believe I can do it again, this time with a person in the wheelbarrow?" The crowd screamed enthusiastically, "Yes! We've seen your work! We believe you can do it again!" Calverly then responded, "Well who wants to go first? Who wants to climb in?" The story goes that no one was willing to get into that wheelbarrow. It was easy to say, "I believe," but their professed belief was not supported by their action.

This gives us a powerful picture of what it means to follow Christ. It's more than just saying, "Yeah, I go to church," or, "Yeah, I believe that some of the stories about Jesus are true." It's saying, "I entrust my life to Jesus as a part of the family of God, and I trust that he's going to take my family on an incredible journey." Then, we act by stepping into the mission with the family of God.

Maybe you have already gotten into the wheelbarrow trusting Jesus and now are asking, "Well, what's my unique call? What am I supposed to do? What does it mean for my family to be on mission as part of the family of God?"

It is about reflecting God where you live, work, and play. Like Jesus, we should be inviting people into the family. Like Jesus, we want to be the kind of people who will live out our purpose, ultimately to glorify God. There's nothing that will glorify God more than living our faith in such a way that invites people into the family of

God. If this is why Jesus came to earth and died on the cross, inviting people into the family of God, then it is our purpose, too. There's no greater purpose. There's no greater mission. And like Jesus, we want to invite people into the family in just a few simple ways.

With a Conversation

Do you realize that a simple conversation could change a person's eternal destiny? Think about the first time you heard that God loves you so much that he gave his only Son so you could be saved. I am sure someone spoke to you. The mission of God is advanced through speaking and hearing. Consider Paul's words in Romans 10:14–15 NLT:

> [14]*How, then, can they call on the one they have not believed in? And how can they believe in the one of whom they have not heard? And how can they hear without someone preaching to them?* [15]*And how can anyone preach unless they are sent? As it is written: "How beautiful are the feet of those who bring good news!"*

God is putting people all around you who need to hear about his love for them. You have neighbors, coworkers, friends, and family members. You don't have to know the answer to every question they might have, because I know that God will give you the right words to speak the truth in love. If you will have in mind the mission of God to reconcile people to himself while you converse with people, you will be amazed at how easily you will be able to share Christ with others.

With Generosity

You want to get somebody's attention? Be a generous person. Go out of your way to be a blessing to people. Invite them into your home. Invite them into a conversation about what's going on in their lives. Invite them to a meal. If you see a need in that person's life, meet that need. If they ask, "Why in the world would you do that?" you can say, "I'm just showing God's love in a practical way."

With Authentic Living

Finally, invite people to experience the family of God with authentic living. Authentic living means being willing to stand up and say, "We're broken, we need a savior, and we're in process," as we are inviting others into that family. Truthfully, our most powerful missional tool is being open and honest about our own imperfections. The world has seen polished religiosity and is not impressed, because it is not honest. If you want to impact others as a family, invite them into your authentic journey to resist sin and live more like Jesus Christ.

Living Connected on Mission

Whom will you invite into the family of God? If you have crossed the line of faith and entered into the family of God, ask God to work on your heart in these areas: anger, conflict, money, words, touch, and rest. You will move from being an isolated, self-focused individual, to becoming a healthy family connected on mission.

After much hard work and with the help of friends and skilled counselors, I feel healthy. I am living

SUMMARY AND INVITATION TO MISSION

more connected to my spouse and kids than ever. I am passionate about "me and my house serving the Lord." I feel confident that when I am nearing my last breath, I will look back over the course of my life and know that I lived well. But, I am still in process. I fail. I stumble. I drift. And, it is okay. The amazing thing about God's grace is that we get to experience his rescue every day until our death. This is good news. I hope you will take the difficult journey into your own past while assessing how you connect with others in your home today. The relationships in your home are worth it. The mission of God through you to others is worth it! Along the way, just know that I am for you, and, more importantly, God is with you as you choose to serve the Lord.

Notes

Chapter 1

1. You can try it yourself at https://www.myabaris.com/tools/life-expectancy-calculator-how-long-will-i-live/.

2. John Piper, *Don't Waste Your Life* (Wheaton, IL: Crossway, 2003), 47–48.

Chapter 2

1. Elizabeth Mostofsky, Elizabeth Anne Penner, and Murray A. Mittleman, "Outbursts of Anger as a Trigger of Acute Cardiovascular Events: A Systematic Review and Meta-analysis," *European Heart Journal* 35, no. 21 (2014), 1404–1410.

2. A synagogue was a Jewish gathering that was very similar to the church in the first century.

3. St. Augustine, *Confessions*, 1.12.

Chapter 3

1. Andrew Newberg and Mark Robert Waldman, *Words Can Change Your Brain* (New York: Penguin, 2013), 3.

2. Andrew Newberg and Mark Robert Waldman, *Words Can Change Your Brain* (New York: Penguin, 2013), 3.

3. Newberg and Waldman, *Words Can Change Your Brain*, 17.
4. Wayne A. Mack, *Your Family, God's Way: Developing and Sustaining Relationships in the Home* (Phillipsburg, NJ: P&R, 1991), 125.

Chapter 4
1. Kerry Patterson, Joseph Grenny, Ron McMillan, and Al Switzler, *Crucial Conversations: Tools for Talking When Stakes Are High* (New York: McGraw Hill, 2002), 13.
2. Sigmund Freud, trans. James Strachey, *Civilization and Its Discontents* (New York: W. W. Norton, 1961), 58–63.
3. A. W. Tozer, *The Pursuit of God* (Camp Hill, PA: Christian Publications, 1993), 90.

Chapter 5
1. David Linden, quoted in Adam Gopnik, "Feel Me," *The New Yorker*, May 16, 2016, http://www.newyorker.com/magazine/2016/05/16/what-the-science-of-touch-says-about-us.
2. Adam Gopnik, "Feel Me."
3. Dacher Keltner, quoted in Adam Gopnik, "Feel Me."
4. Tiffany Field, *Touch* (Cambridge: MIT, 2014), 7.
5. Steven Tracy and Celestia Tracy, *Forever and Always: The Art of Intimacy* (Eugene, OR: Wipf & Stock, 2011), 106–108.

NOTES

6. Dawn Nelson, *From the Heart through the Hands: The Power of Touch in Caregiving* (Findhorn, Scotland: Findhorn Press, 2006).

7. Daniel Goleman, "The Experience of Touch: Research Points to a Critical Role," *The New York Times*, Feb. 2, 1988, http://www.nytimes.com/1988/02/02/science/the-experience-of-touch-research-points-to-a-critical-role.html.

8. Much could be said about how to do this and why it is increasingly difficult in our culture. Others (like Steven and Celestia Tracy in *Forever and Always: The Art of Intimacy*) have treated this subject more thoroughly than I am able to in this work, and I recommend you put in some time to learn how to touch your spouse in healthy ways.

9. Steven Tracy and Celestia Tracy, *Forever and Always: The Art of Intimacy*, 108.

10. Joseph S. Alpert, "Philematology: The Science of Kissing. A Message for the Marital Month of June," *The American Journal of Medicine* 126, no. 6 (2013): 466.

11. See also Steven Tracy and Celestia Tracy, *Forever and Always*; along with Tim Keller and Kathy Keller, *The Meaning of Marriage* (New York: Penguin, 2011).

12. Steven Tracy and Celestia Tracy, *Forever and Always: The Art of Intimacy*, 106–108.

Chapter 6

1. See Andy Walton, "Creflo Dollar Removes Facebook Post which Claims Jesus Died to Give Us 'Financial Prosperity,'" *Christianity Today*, Oct. 9, 2015, https://www.christiantoday.com/article/creflo.dollar.removes.facebook.post.which.claims.jesus.died.to.give.us.financial.prosperity/67092.htm.
2. I recommend a tool called EveryDollar (https://www.everydollar.com/) to those who are trying to build a budget for the first time.

Chapter 7

1. "Waiting for Our Souls to Catch Up," Storiesforpreaching.com, https://storiesforpreaching.com/waiting-for-our-souls-to-catch-up/.
2. E. J. Young, F. F. Bruce, "Sabbath," in D. R. W. Wood, I. H. Marshall, A. R. Millard, J. I. Packer, and D. J. Wiseman, eds., *New Bible Dictionary*, 3rd ed. (Downers Grove, IL: InterVarsity Press, 1996), 1032.
3. St. Augustine, *Confessions*, 1.1.2.
4. Craig Keener, *The IVP Bible Background Commentary: New Testament* (Downers Grove, IL: InterVarsity Press).
5. Brady Boyd, *Addicted to Busy: Recovery for the Rushed Soul* (Colorado Springs, CO: David C. Cook, 2014), 83.
6. Just to be clear, I am a firm believer in the need for regular Bible study.
7. R. K. Harrison, "Feasts and Festivals of Israel," in *The Baker Encyclopedia of the Bible*, vol. 1 (Grand Rapids, MI: Baker, 1988), 783.

CPSIA information can be obtained
at www.ICGtesting.com
Printed in the USA
FFOW03n0109040118
44341905-44011FF